2 SAMUEL
FOR YOU

TIM CHESTER
2 SAMUEL
FOR YOU

thegoodbook
COMPANY

2 Samuel For You

© Tim Chester/The Good Book Company, 2017. Reprinted 2021.

Published by:
The Good Book Company

thegoodbook.com | thegoodbook.co.uk
thegoodbook.com.au | thegoodbook.co.nz | thegoodbook.co.in

ISBN: 9781784981990

Design by André Parker | Printed in Turkey

CONTENTS

Bible translations used:

- NIV: New International Version, 2011 translation (this is the version being quoted unless otherwise stated)

- ESV: English Standard Version

- NASB: New American Standard Bible

SERIES PREFACE

Each volume of the *God's Word For You* series takes you to the heart of a book of the Bible, and applies its truths to your heart.

The central aim of each title is to be:

- Bible centred
- Christ glorifying
- Relevantly applied
- Easily readable

You can use *2 Samuel For You:*

To read. You can simply read from cover to cover, as a book that explains and explores the themes, encouragements and challenges of this part of Scripture.

To feed. You can work through this book as part of your own personal regular devotions, or use it alongside a sermon or Bible-study series at your church. Each chapter is divided into two shorter sections, with questions for reflection at the end of each.

To lead. You can use this as a resource to help you teach God's word to others, both in small-group and whole-church settings. You'll find tricky verses or concepts explained using ordinary language, and helpful themes and illustrations along with suggested applications.

These books are not commentaries. They assume no understanding of the original Bible languages, nor a high level of biblical knowledge. Verse references are marked in **bold** so that you can refer to them easily. Any words that are used rarely or differently in everyday language outside the church are marked in grey when they first appear, and are explained in a glossary towards the back. There, you'll also find details of resources you can use alongside this one, in both personal and church life.

Our prayer is that as you read, you'll be struck not by the contents of this book, but by the book it's helping you open up; and that you'll praise not the author of this book, but the One he is pointing you to.

Carl Laferton, Series Editor

INTRODUCTION TO 2 SAMUEL

2 Samuel is full of action. We lurch from one dramatic moment to another. We move from victory to defeat and back to victory; from civil war to national victory and back to civil war again. We read of domestic dramas and national crises; miraculous interventions and faithful suffering. The big beasts of Israelite politics square off against one another on numerous occasions. It can all be somewhat breathless.

But this is no simple fairy tale with characters drawn in black and white. Alongside all the action is a good deal of ambiguity. Yes, we meet heroes and villains. But more often we meet people somewhere in between. We encounter heroic loyalty and treacherous betrayals. We find people whose lives are both good and bad, ugly and beautiful, selfless and self-serving—people like us.

But through it all we see the hand of God, the true hero of the story. David sings a song at the end of his life in 2 Samuel 22. At the beginning, in the middle and at the end is the affirmation, "The LORD is my rock". It's the refrain of the song and it's the refrain of David's life.

For David is God's anointed king. The word for "anointed One" in Hebrew is "messiah" and in Greek it's "christ". So David is God's christ (small "c")—his anointed king. It means 2 Samuel is a mirror in which we see Jesus, the ultimate Christ (capital "C"). Again and again the story of 2 Samuel enables us to see the glory of Christ. When David is strong and faithful and victorious, he prefigures the strength and faithfulness and victory of Jesus. When David is selfish and faithless, we feel our need for a better king—the kind of king we see in David's greater Son. And sometimes, when David is weak and beset by troubles, we see the suffering of Jesus, the Good Shepherd who died for his people.

In David's final words he says:

"When one rules over people in righteousness,
    when he rules in the fear of God,

> he is like the light of morning at sunrise
>
> on a cloudless morning,
>
> like the brightness after rain
>
> that brings grass from the earth." (2 Samuel 23:3-4)

This is David's philosophy of kingship—the "mission statement" of David's monarchy. But it only truly finds fulfilment in Jesus, the true Son of David. As you read 2 Samuel, look out for the "the light of morning at sunrise … the brightness after rain that brings grass from the earth" as you see the glory of Christ reflected in the story of his ancestor David.

Two Notes on the Book

Who wrote the books of 1 and 2 Samuel? The short answer is that we do not know. They are named after the prophet Samuel, but this does not mean he wrote them. In the Greek version of the Old Testament, they are called "1 and 2 Kingdoms". And Samuel's death is described in 1 Samuel 25:1, so he could not have written about the events after this point. Nevertheless, Samuel may have been one source for the books; 1 Chronicles 29:29 talks about "the records of Samuel the seer". The books were probably compiled from different sources.

Again and again the story of 2 Samuel enables us to see the glory of Christ.

And what kind of genre is this? A useful description is that this is a *preached history*. In other words, it is real history. It is not a collection of parables or fables—the events it describes really did happen. But it is more than a record of events. 1 Chronicles 29:29 says: "As for the events of King David's reign, from beginning to end, they are written in the records of Samuel the seer, the records of Nathan the prophet and the records of Gad the seer."

There were other historical annals. The writer of Samuel is doing more than creating a historical record. He is writing with a purpose. What he records is never less than historical, but as we read it, we are doing much more than reading history. We are being shown who God is and how he rules his people; and we are being shown Jesus, his Christ.

1. THE MESS OF HISTORY

What is God doing in the world today? The central claim of Christianity is that Jesus is Lord. But that claim seems laughable. Where's the evidence? It doesn't seem as if *anyone* is in control, let alone Jesus. Maybe you long for friends to be saved, you long for the church to grow, you long for justice to be done, you long for the Christ to be honoured. But people continue to ignore the Christ. The media mocks Christianity. **Tyrants**† act with apparent **impunity**. The world is in a mess.

Long ago God rescued his people Israel from slavery in Egypt through **Moses**. He gave them the promised land through **Joshua**. Then about 1,000 years BC they asked for a king. So **Saul** was chosen and became the king of Israel. His reign started well, but he decided to disobey God. So God told the prophet **Samuel** to **anoint** David as his successor. Saul got wind of this and so for many years David lived as a fugitive as Saul tried to hunt down the rival to his throne. The book of 1 Samuel ended with Saul, facing defeat in battle, committing suicide.

2 Samuel 1 – 5 tells the story of the transition from the end of Saul's reign to David's enthronement as king over all Israel. And frankly *it's a mess*. It's not a neat transfer of power. It's not even clear who are the good guys. It's the story of David and his army commander, Joab, and Ish-Bosheth, Saul's son, and his army commander, Abner. Who are the good guys? Judge for yourself.

---

† Words in **grey** are defined in the Glossary (page 169).

The story is arranged in a **chiastic** structure (a common Hebrew literary device in which the second half of story or poem mirrors the first half):

a. David executes the (purported) murderer of Saul (**1:1-16***)

   b. David laments Saul and **Jonathan** (**1:17-27**)

      c. A struggle between the houses of David and Saul (**2:1 – 3:1**)

         d. David's house (**3:2-5**)

      c*. A struggle between Abner and Joab (**3:6-30**)

   b*. David **laments** Abner (**3:31-39**)

a*. David executes the murderers of Ish-Bosheth, Saul's son (**4:1-12**)

David Executes a Murderer

2 Samuel begins with an **Amalekite** coming from the battlefield to David and honouring him as king (**1:1-2**). When he comes to David, David repeats **Eli's** question after a previous battle with the **Philistines**: "What happened?" (1 Samuel 4:16; 2 Samuel **1:4**). The first question marked the end of a priestly house; the second, the end of a royal house.

The Amalekite tells David that Saul is dead (**v 3-4**). "How do you know?" asks David (**v 5**). *Because I killed him,* is basically what the man says in reply (**v 6-10**). We know from 1 Samuel 31 (as presumably David did not) the story of Saul's death. So, as the Amalekite recounts the story, we realise his version is different. This is reinforced by the threefold repetition of "the young man who brought this report" (2 Samuel **1:5, 6, 13**). The narrator keeps reminding us that this is only his "report" and not necessarily the facts.

The young man claims that it was he (and not Saul) who delivered the final blow (**v 4-9**). "I happened to be" on a battlefield stretches credibility (**v 6**). More likely he was **scavenging** among the dead. Now he has brought the crown and royal armband to David, expecting to be

---

* All 2 Samuel verse references being looked at in each chapter are in **bold**.

well rewarded for his actions (**v 10**). He assumes David is desperate to become king and will be delighted with the man who paves the way. But the narrator has already hinted that this will not go well for this Amalekite, for David has just returned from "striking down the Amale-kites" (**v 1**).

But we also know from 1 Samuel that David has consistently *re-fused* to snatch the crown from Saul. Indeed David was conscience-stricken after merely cutting off the corner Saul's robe (1 Samuel 24:5). "Why weren't you afraid to lift your hand to destroy the LORD's anointed?" he asks in genuine puzzlement (2 Samuel **1:14**). David checks his background (**v 13**). "The son of a foreigner" is the term for a sojourner, a Gentile who had made his home among God's people. In other words, David checks this Amalekite understands the import of what he claims to have done. In **verses 15-16** David orders, "Go, strike him down" (echoing **verse 1**). The irony is, of course, that the young man didn't kill Saul. He loses his life for a lie.

Saul lost his kingdom because he plundered the Amalekites, against God's strict orders. Now an Amalekite has plundered him. Saul claimed to have wiped out the Amalekites, but he did not (1 Samuel 15:8-9, 13; 28:18). Now an Amalekite claims to have wiped out Saul, but he did not. More significant are the opening words of 2 Samuel:

"After the death of Saul, David returned from striking down the Amalekites and stayed in **Ziklag** two days" *(*1:1*)*.

Saul died because he failed to strike down the Amalekites, and so the christ of Israel (her anointed king) is dead. Immediately, David returns to centre stage. And what has he been doing? Striking down Amale-kites. The message is clear: *He is the christ that Saul was not.*

On the first Good Friday the ultimate Christ died—not for his diso-bedience, but for ours. And hope was gone. But two days later (on "the third day") Christ returned. Paul asserts that Christ rose on the third day "according to the Scriptures" (1 Corinthians 15:4). Perhaps the words "on the third day" in 2 Samuel **1:2** in the context of David's rise to kingship is one prophetic pointer towards that claim.

David Laments Saul and Jonathan

David does not rejoice that his adversary is dead. Instead, he and his men respond with impromptu grief (**v 11-12**). This is followed later by a composed song of lament for Saul and his son Jonathan (**v 17-27**). Saul may have been a rogue, but he was the king of Israel.

Imagine a prime minister or president whom you personally dislike is assassinated. You would naturally respond with shock, outrage and sadness. We honour the post, even if we don't honour the post-holder. This is not the time to linger on Saul's faults. David proclaims his virtues along with the more evident virtues of Jonathan (**v 19, 22-24**). He doesn't want Israel's enemies to hear the news (**v 20-21**). He adds his own personal grief at the loss of his friend Jonathan (**v 25-26**).

Verse 21 creates a tragic image. Shields were often covered with leather, which needed to be oiled. But "the shield of Saul" now lies in the dust. But Saul, too, was anointed with oil as God's king to be a shield for the people. Now the shield-which-is-Saul lies in the dust. **Verse 22** celebrates Jonathan's bow and Saul's sword, which have been features of the story (1 Samuel 20:20, 36 and 17:38-39). Were Saul and Jonathan undivided as 2 Samuel **1:23** suggests? Not always. Saul twice tried to kill his son (1 Samuel 14:39, 44; 20:33-34). But Jonathan remained loyal and died fighting alongside his father (2 Samuel **1:23**).

The phrase "your love for me was wonderful, more wonderful than that of women" in **verse 26** has been taken to suggest a homosexual relationship between David and Jonathan. But in a military culture and a culture in which marriage could be a matter of political expedience, the bonds between fellow warriors might well be deeply felt. The suggestion, in fact, says more about our own culture's sexualisation of relationships.

The Struggle Between the Houses

In **2:1-4** the men of the tribe of Judah anoint David as king. This section starts with David "enquiring" of the LORD. The Hebrew word has the same root as "Saul". Saul was the king the people had "asked for", but Saul himself did not "ask of" the LORD as now David does.

Hebron was a key location in the story of the **Patriarchs** and the place of their burial. God's choice of this location links David's story to **Abraham's** (as Matthew 1:1 does). David is fulfilling the promises made to Abraham: through David God's people will live in the land under God's blessing (2 Samuel 7:1).

Throughout the period of the **judges** and into Saul's reign, the tribes of Israel had remained to a large degree like independent political entities. They were more like the nation states making up the European Union than counties in the nation of Great Britain. So for one tribe to acknowledge David as king did not mean he was king of Israel, especially as that one tribe was his own.

The men of Jabesh Gilead were allied to Saul. We might suppose they would be David's natural enemies. But David commends them because they showed kindness or **covenant** loyalty to Saul (**2:4-5**). David prays that God will show the same kindness and covenant loyalty to them (**v 6-7**). David is king, but he is keen to heal the divisions in the kingdom by honouring those who have honoured his predecessor. He is a picture of Jesus, who rises victorious to offer grace to his enemies—those allied to Satan.

> Abner knew David was God's anointed... but he rejects him.

But David's **accession** is not going to be straightforward. While David is being crowned by the tribe of Judah, Abner, Saul's army commander, is crowning Ish-Bosheth, Saul's son (**v 8-11**). Abner knew David was God's anointed—he would have heard Saul acknowledge as much in 1 Samuel 24:20 and 26:25. But he rejects him. David is God's anointed. Ish-Bosheth is Abner's anointed.

The result is a stand-off between the armies of Abner and Joab (**2:12-13**). "Abner said to Joab, 'Now let the young men arise and hold a contest before us'" (**v 14**, NASB). The word "contest" is normally used for play. It shares the same root as "laughter". It's the word behind **Isaac's** name (Genesis 21:3-6). The same word is used to describe the Philistines bringing **Samson** out in the temple of **Dagon** for their "amusement" (Judges 16:25-27). It seems Abner is suggesting a tournament somewhat akin to the medieval tournaments in which knights proved their prowess.

But this tournament turns deadly. At the end of Shakespeare's *Hamlet*, Prince Hamlet and Laertes have a sporting dual, but Laertes has secretly poisoned the end of his sword so the dual turns from being fun to being fatal—especially as they swap swords in the course of their fight. In 2 Samuel 2 both sides are intent on deadly betrayal and so both fall victim to the other.

The fight is clearly intended to be symbolic. Perhaps Abner intended it as a non-deadly version of Goliath's challenge in 1 Samuel 17, a winner-takes-all combat. Perhaps the hope was that this military diversion would create time for a political solution. But we have a divided Israel "Isaacing" to determine who are the true sons of Abraham. Each side is represented by twelve men fighting to determine who are the true tribes of Israel.

What is the result? All 24 fall in a bizarre, almost synchronised, act of simultaneous mutual stabbing (2 Samuel **2:15-16**). The true Israel will not be determined by civil war. Sadly, Abner and Joab do not pick up on the clues and a brutal civil war is what follows (**v 17**).

Joab wins the battle and Abner is forced to flee, pursued by Asahel, Joab's brother. Asahel is described as being "as fleet-footed as a wild **gazelle**" (**v 18-19**), which may not bode well for him since the last person likened to a gazelle lies fallen on the heights of Israel (**1:19**). Abner does all he can to avoid fighting Asahel (**2:20-22**), but Asahel refuses to give up his pursuit. So eventually Abner kills Asahel by thrusting the butt of his spear through his stomach (**v 23**). Joab corners Abner, but Benjaminite warriors rally round Abner (**v 24-25**). Things look set for a bloody showdown. But then Abner says, "Must the sword devour for ever? Don't you realise that this will end in bitterness? How long before you order your men to stop pursuing their fellow Israelites?" (**v 26**) Joab sees the sense of this and calls off the pursuit (**v 27-32**).

"The war between the house of Saul and the house of David lasted a long time," we are told in **3:1**. Earlier we were told that Ish-Bosheth reigned for two years (**2:10**). But throughout this period "David grew stronger and stronger, while the house of Saul grew weaker and weaker" (**3:1**).

> David grew stronger and stronger, while the house of Saul grew weaker and weaker.

David's Dangerous House

These verses are at the centre of the chiastic structure—and often that means they are the most significant. Yet in dramatic terms they are the least exciting. We meet a similar summary at the end (the climax?) of this section in 5:13-16. It may be intended to signify the power of David, with his sexual potency mirroring his growing political potency. But at a political level, the multiplication of sons bodes ill for the future. David has six sons, each by a different mother. Already the succession is looking complicated. At a spiritual level, it sets an example to his sons which will reap still further disasters for God's people (1 Kings 11:1-13).

What appears expedient in the moment can often have disastrous long-term results. And that is as true in parenting as with anything else. Think about your own parenting, if you have children. A repeated failure to enact discipline because you're tired or in a hurry, or the expedient act which is a bad example, may reap bitter fruit in years to come.

Questions for reflection

1. The setting at the start of 2 Samuel is one of conflict. What hostility or conflict do you face in your everyday life? How can you understand the causes of those conflicts, pray about them, and work to resolve them in light of what we have read so far?

2. War, scheming, lies and brutal murder are all described here, and yet from this mess, God's chosen king is slowly raised up to power. How can we reconcile these gritty facts of history with the belief that a good God is in control of all things?

3. How does this passage suggest we should pray for our world, our church, and our leaders?

PART TWO

A Struggle Between Abner and Joab

Often in times of war, it is the generals who profit and so it was in Israel: "During the war between the house of Saul and the house of David, Abner had been strengthening his own position in the house of Saul" (2 Samuel **3:6**). Ish-Bosheth accuses Abner of taking a royal **concubine**, a political crime signifying **usurpation** as much as a sexual crime (**v 7**). But there is no indication that Abner is guilty of the charge, and he responds with an angry defence of his loyalty (**v 8-10**). Whether Abner is guilty or not, Ish-Bosheth is too weak to press his claim (**v 11**).

Slighted by Ish-Bosheth, Abner switches sides and pursues a negotiated peace (**v 12**). David agrees as long as Abner delivers his estranged wife, Saul's daughter, Michal (**v 13-14**). Abner lobbies the elders of Israel to persuade them to back David (**v 17-18**). We are told "Abner also spoke to the **Benjaminites** in person", presumably because Saul was a Benjaminite so they needed extra persuasion (**v 19**). With the backing of Israel secured, Abner goes to Hebron and the deal is sealed with a feast (**v 20-21**).

The final word of **verse 21** is important: "peace". Three times we are told that David sent Abner away in peace (**v 21-23**). Peace at last. Or so it seems.

The problem is that when Joab finds out about the deal, he's furious (**v 23-25**). He professes concern for David's safety (**v 24-25**), but it may be he fears that Abner will replace him as David's commander-in-chief. He also wants revenge for the death of his brother (**v 30**). So Joab sends messengers after Abner and arranges a private meeting (**v 26**). Abner assumes Joab is on David's business. But Joab has his own business in mind. Abner left in peace. But Joab calls him back to Hebron, an ancient **City of Refuge** where Abner should have found safety (Joshua 20). But it is not peace or refuge that Abner finds. Abner had killed Joab's brother with a stomach wound, but that had been in battle. Now Joab kills Abner with a stomach wound, but he takes him by surprise and kills him in cold blood (2 Samuel **3:26-27**).

A Lament for Abner

When David hears of Abner's assassination he immediately repudiates the act: "I and my kingdom are for ever innocent before the LORD concerning the blood of Abner son of Ner" (**v 28**). He then publicly signals this innocence in a variety of ways:

- David condemns Joab with a fivefold curse (**v 29**).

- David commands Joab to wear the clothes of mourning and walk in front of Abner's bier (**v 31**).

- David himself walks behind the bier and leads the people in their weeping for Abner (**v 31-32**).

- David composes a lament for Abner (**v 33-34**).

- David refuses to eat (**v 35**).

- David disowns Joab and his brothers (**v 38-39**).

Abner had led the army of Israel for many years, so no doubt much of this was genuine. But it was also politically **expedient**. It worked well as a PR exercise. Seven times in **verses 31-37** the writer refers to "all the people" (a fact which is clearer in the ESV than the NIV). "All the people took note and were pleased; indeed, everything the king did pleased them. So on that day all the people there and all Israel knew that the king had no part in the murder of Abner son of Ner" (**v 36-37**). But David is too weak to do anything about Joab (**v 38-39**)—that he will leave to his son Solomon (1 Kings 2:5-6, 28-35). Literally, David is "gentle" (Matthew 11:29) while Joab is a "hard" man.

David Executes the Murderer of Ish-Bosheth

The peace deal falls through, but without Abner the writing is on the wall for Ish-Bosheth (2 Samuel **4:1**). Nevertheless his end is still ignominious. He is killed by two of his own men, as the writer is keen to establish (**v 2-3**). Baanah and Rekab murder Ish-Bosheth while he is taking his noonday rest (**v 5-6**). Hebrew narratives quite often repeat descriptions of events with added details the second time round. **Verse 7** repeats **verses 5-6** but adds the facts that they killed Ish-Bosheth while he was lying down, and that they cut off his head off after they had killed him with a stomach wound.

Both facts are significant. The killing of a man while he is lying down—and perhaps still asleep—highlights the fact that this is not an act of war, but an assassination. This is cold-blooded murder. This is why David calls Ish-Bosheth "innocent". His life was not innocent, but his death was because it wasn't a judicial act.

Cutting off Ish-Bosheth's head parallels the death of his father. Both are struck in the stomach and then beheaded. Both their deaths are reported

> Literally David is "gentle" while Joab is a "hard" man.

to David by people who think they will earn his favour, but in fact are executed for their crime. Ish-Bosheth's death is also similar to that of Abner. Both are murdered in an inner room through a stomach wound by brothers.

Baanah and Rekab bring Ish-Bosheth's severed head to David thinking they will be well rewarded (**v 8**). But they badly miscalculate David's loyalties—just as the Amalekite did in chapter 1. Indeed David himself draws the parallels (**v 9-10**). So David has the men executed for killing an innocent man in his bed (**v 11-12**).

Who Are the Good Guys in This Story?

Abner is a mix of self-sacrificial loyalty and self-interested power-broking. He makes Ish-Bosheth king rather than himself and he does all he can to avoid killing Asahel. But he also knows that God has anointed David as Saul's successor (**3:9, 18**). Yet still he sides with Ish-Bosheth in opposition not only to David, but to God himself. **2:11** says David was king of Judah in Hebron for seven and a half years. But Ish-Bosheth was only king for two years (**v 10**). This suggests Abner did not appoint Ish-Bosheth immediately in response to Saul's death, but five years into David's reign when he had calculated that his interests lay with Ish-Bosheth.

But when those calculations change, he changes, and switches sides. We only have Ish-Bosheth's word for the accusation that Abner took one of Saul's concubines. But we are told that "Abner had been strengthening his own position in the house of Saul" (**3:6**). His question to David in **v 12**, "Whose land is it?" implies the answer "Mine". Abner presents himself as the power-broker who can give the land to whomever he chooses. In the end he is a warlord.

Joab and his brothers are often known as "the sons of Zeruiah" (**2:18**; **3:39**; 16:10; 19:22). This is a common enough way of describing someone in the Old Testament. David is often called "the son of Jesse". But what makes this different is that Zeruiah is their *mother* rather than their father (17:25; 1 Chronicles 2:16). Joab seems genuinely committed to David. But he is also committed to his own interests.

Joab's hostility to Abner is both personal and political. He blames Abner for the loss of his brother (2 Samuel **3:30**), but he also knows Abner's alliance with David will lead to him losing his position as the army commander. So he kills Abner in cold blood. Like Abner, Joab is a warlord.

Ish-Bosheth was a nickname. His real name was Ish-Baal or Esh-Baal (1 Chronicles 8:33; 9:39). "**Baal**" means "husband" or "lord". So Ish-Baal means "man of the husband" (perhaps a reference to the king as a husband to the nation) or "man of the lord". ·

But Baal was also a name of the **Canaanite** gods. So the writer of Samuel substitutes "Bosheth" for "Baal" (he also does this with Mephibosheth who is Merib-Baal in 1 Chronicles 8:34; 9:40) to create Ish-Bosheth—"man of shame". And indeed he is a rather pitiful figure. The first time he is mentioned we're told, "Abner son of Ner, the commander of Saul's army, had taken Ish-Bosheth son of Saul and brought him over to Mahanaim. He made him king" (2 Samuel **2:8-9**). Notice the verbs: "taken", "brought" and "made". Ish-Bosheth is entirely passive. These events happen to him. He is not the agent of his future. He is a puppet in the hands of Abner. The only time he initiates anything is in his accusation that Abner has taken Saul's concubine. But he lacks the power to follow it through. "Ish-Bosheth did not dare to say another word to Abner, because he was afraid of him" (**3:11**). His reign starts (and soon ends) as Saul's ended, with him being king in name only and without real power.

David works hard to heal the nation. He executes the purported murderer of Saul and honours Saul in song. He commends the men of Jabesh-Gilead for burying Saul in a dignified way. He jumps at the opportunity offered him by Abner to take the throne without bloodshed (**v 6-21**). He distances himself from the murder of Abner and mourns his death. He executes the men who murdered Ish-Bosheth. Later he locates his capital, Jerusalem, in the territory of **Benjamin**, the tribe of Saul (Joshua 18:28).

But David is also flawed. First, he fails to deal with Joab. He disowns Joab's actions, but does not punish them. David felt Joab was too powerful for him to punish (2 Samuel **3:38-39**). He was perhaps also influenced by the ties of blood, for Joab was his nephew, one of the sons of David's sister, Zeruiah (1 Chronicles 2:13-16). The weakness of David's punishment of Joab

> David works hard to heal the nation… but David is also flawed.

in 2 Samuel **3:28-29** is highlighted by the strength of the punishment of Rekab and Baanah even though their crime (killing an innocent man) is the same. David deals with the murderers of Ish-Bosheth and the purported murderer of Saul, but not with the murderer of Abner.

Second, David commits **polygamy** (**v 2-5, 13-16;** 5:13-16). This sows the seeds of future problems. David's demand for the return of Michal may also have been driven by a desire to unite the nation (**3:13-14**). Michal was Saul's daughter and David's former wife who, after David's break with Saul, had been given by her father to another husband. David may have hoped that he and Michal could have a son who would unite the two houses. If so, the hope was ill-conceived. A marriage divided between many wives was not a good basis for a united state.

The text emphasises the distress of Paltiel, Michal's husband (**v 15-16**). Paltiel's divided family does not bode for a united kingdom. And so it proves. Michal and David become estranged and she remains childless (6:20-23). 1 Samuel 18:20 says Michal was in love with David. It is the only time in the Old Testament we are explicitly told of a woman's love for a man. But her love became the victim of male power-politics. Now again she is torn from a man who loves her because she is caught up in male power-politics. Rather than bringing joy to Israel, this act brings sorrow. The list of David's wives and concubines in 2 Samuel 5:13-16 begins, "David took". It is an ominous echo of 1 Samuel 8:11-17, where Samuel warns Israel that future kings "will take your sons ... will take your daughters ... will take a tenth of your grain ... Your male and female servants and the best of your cattle and donkeys he will take for his own use. He will take a tenth of your flocks, and you yourselves will become his slaves."

> The key player is not Abner, Joab or David. The key player is God.

The Key Player

Who are the good guys in this story? It's far from clear. In fact it all looks like a big mess. These chapters are full of brutal fights and underhand betrayals. We can debate the morality of the various key players. But perhaps that misses the point. This is not a morality tale.

It is part of the story of **redemption**. The key player is not Abner, Joab or David. The key player is God, and in the next chapter we'll explore what God is doing through the mess of history. In the meantime, we see the danger of investing our hopes in human heroes.

Questions for reflection

1. Hero or villain? Goodie or baddie? Why is it unhelpful to have this simplistic view of humankind?

2. The weakness and failure of these "heroes" makes us hunger for the one true hero—Jesus. How does the Lord Jesus succeed in comparable areas, where these people failed?

3. How can we encourage ourselves to trust in God's sovereign purposes when life is a mess?

2. THE LORD EXALTS

I was once catching a plane from Manchester airport. I had just put my belt and bag in the plastic tray to go through the x-ray machine. As I turned to walk through the security scanner, I realised the person in the line next to me was Patrick Vieira, one-time captain of **Arsenal** Football Club and part of the French soccer team that won the World Cup in 1998. What struck me was how big he was: he's 6'4" (1.8m). He must have been very imposing on a football pitch. He was pretty imposing in an airport. "After you," I said. "No, after you," he replied. I did as I was told.

Compare this with Gianfranco Zola, the former **Chelsea** footballer. When he played in the UK's Premier League, commentators would always append the word "little" to his name: he's 5'6"(1.5m). "The ball is played out to little Zola. He cuts inside and shoots ... What a goal from the little man!"

Tall and Small

We have something similar in 1 and 2 Samuel. The first time we meet Saul, we're told, "He was a head taller than anyone else" (1 Samuel 9:2). He is literally head and shoulders above the rest. He is the tallest man in Israel. When Saul disobeys God, God anoints a replacement: David. And when we first meet David he's described as "the young-est" of **Jesse's** sons (1 Samuel 16:11). It's literally the "smallest". So the two main **protagonists** in the story are tall Saul and little David. Saul is tallest and David is the smallest.

This is not incidental. It embodies one of the central themes of the books of 1 and 2 Samuel. 1 Samuel started with the song of **Hannah**.

Hannah reflects on her own experience of being childless and then having a child. She sees her experience as a picture of God's plan for his people. So her song sets the agenda for the books as a whole. Hannah sang, "The LORD will … exalt the **horn** of his anointed"—the power of his christ (1 Samuel 2:10). This is what God is doing in the story. David is the christ, God's anointed, and through this story he becomes king. Hannah also sang, "The LORD … brings low and he exalts." (2:7, ESV). Behind all the political intrigue and scheming of 2 Samuel 1 – 4, we see the LORD bringing low the house of Saul and exalting the house of David.

"The LORD Brings Low"—the Fall of Tall Saul

The book of Samuel begins and end with song—the song of Hannah in 1 Samuel 2 and the song of David in 2 Samuel 22. In the middle is the lament David composes on the death of Saul and Jonathan. Its refrain is this: "How the mighty have fallen!" (1:19, 25, 27). 1 Samuel 31 says Saul "fell" on his sword (v 4), his armour bearer "fell" on his sword (v 5), and the Philistines found Saul and his sons "fallen" on Mount Gilboa (v 8). And the word "fell" or "fallen" is repeated in 2 Samuel 1:4, 10 and 12.

The distinguishing physical feature of Saul was his height (1 Samuel 9:1). But now he has been brought low. Tall Saul has fallen.

David's lament for Saul in 2 Samuel 1:17-27 starts with a gazelle. It's probably a reference to Jonathan's finest hour, when almost single-handedly he assaulted a Philistine outpost after climbing up a cliff on his hands and knees (1 Samuel 14:13). No doubt it was a rather un-dignified crawl, but David presents it as the light-footed leaping of a gazelle. David recalls the determination of Saul and Jonathan in battle (2 Samuel 2:22) and likens them to eagles and lions (v 23).

But now they are fallen, and David curses the site of their fall (v 21). In verse 20 David wants to censor the news so that the women of **Philistia** do not rejoice at Saul's death. The early church father **Chrysostom** took this as a mandate to not spread the news of another Christian's failure: "If David did not wish the matter paraded in public so that it might not be a source of joy to his foes, so much the more must we avoid spreading the story to alien ears" (*Against Judaising Christians* 8.4.10). Verse 24 presents the other side of this as David calls on the women of Israel to lament Saul's death. Shields were anointed with oil to make them gleam. But Saul's shield has lost its anointing—like Saul himself (v 21). His shield (a picture of his authority) is messiah-less.

> What distinguished Saul was his height. But now he has been brought low.

Chapter 4:1 says Ish-Bosheth "lost courage". It's literally "his hand became slack". He lost his grip on power, we might say. In chapter 4 the house of Saul consists of a slack hand (4:1), crippled feet (v 4) and a severed head (v 7-8). The **body politic** has disintegrated.

"The LORD ... Exalts"—the Rise of Little David

This is the key to understanding history. History is complicated and messy. That complication and mess are fully represented in 2 Samuel 1 – 4. But in the midst of this "the LORD will ... exalt the horn of his anointed" (1 Samuel 2:10). It took 20 chapters, and sometimes David doubted it would ever happen (27:1). But we finally reach the point at the beginning of 2 Samuel 5 where he is crowned. In the midst of all this bloodshed, David is already repeatedly being called "the king" (3:32, 33, 36, 37, 38, 39). Little David has been lifted up.

In **5:1-3** David is anointed as king by "all the tribes of Israel" (**v 1**) and by "all the elders of Israel (**v 3**). We are immediately given a summary of his 40-year reign (**v 4-5**). David then conquers Jerusalem to make his capital city (**v 9**). The **Jebusites** taunt David with the claims that even "the blind and lame can ward you off" (**v 6**). In **verse 8** David says he hates the blind and lame. He's not being prejudiced against people with disabilities (see chapter 9; see also Jesus and his apostles, Matthew 21:14; Acts 3:1-10). He's turning the Jebusite taunts back on them as he captures the city (2 Samuel **5:7**). Jerusalem becomes his capital.

Moving his capital from Hebron may have been a conciliatory act, because Jerusalem was in the territory of Benjamin, Saul's tribe. It may be that David saw himself as a new **Melchizedek**, the Priest-King of Salem (Jerusalem), whom Abraham honoured in Genesis 14:18-20) (a link made in Psalm 110 and Hebrews 7). Certainly David is immediately honoured by other kings (2 Samuel **5:11**) and is able to conclude "that the LORD had established him as king over Israel and had exalted his kingdom for the sake of his people Israel" (**v 12**).

> David is God's anointed king. He is the christ—a picture and pointer to Jesus, the Christ.

Through all the machinations of history, God works to establish his messiah. For that is who David is. "Messiah" or "christ" means "anointed one". And David is God's anointed king. He is the christ—a picture and pointer to Jesus, the Christ.

Perhaps the best commentary on this story is Psalm 2. In the New Testament this psalm is attributed to David (Acts 4:25) and it was probably written as a coronation anthem. Perhaps it was first written to mark the events of 2 Samuel 1 – 5. Or perhaps it was sung every time a new king was crowned.

"Why do the nations conspire
   and the peoples plot in vain?
The kings of the earth rise up,
   and the rulers band together,
   against the LORD and against his anointed, saying,
'Let us break their chains
   and throw off their shackles.'" (Psalm 2:1-3)

In Psalm 2 humanity (represented by the kings of the earth) plot against the LORD and his anointed. They say, "Let us break their chains and throw off their shackles". This is not merely a description of ancient history. This describes our society. It describes our lives. This is what happened in Genesis 3, when Adam and Eve rejected God's rule. And this has been the common characteristic of humanity ever since. We don't want God's rule. We want to run our own lives.

This is what happened in 1 Samuel 8. The people of Israel were not content with God as King. They wanted their own king. And this is what happened in 2 Samuel 2. Abner didn't want to hand over power to God's anointed. He was the commander of the army and he wanted to remain as commander. He wanted Ish-Bosheth as his puppet king. That's why he switched sides so readily. He wanted power. Meanwhile Joab didn't want to hand over power to Abner. So he assassinated Abner. Humanity rejects God's rule in favour of our own self-rule.

How does God respond?

"The One enthroned in heaven laughs;
   the Lord scoffs at them.
He rebukes them in his anger
   and terrifies them in his wrath, saying,
'I have installed my king
   on Zion, my holy mountain.'" (Psalm 2:4-6)

In Psalm 2 God laughs from heaven. This rebellion does not leave him anxious. He's not cowering in fear behind the gates of heaven. He mocks our pretensions. And he asserts that he will install his king.

And this, too, is what happens in 2 Samuel 1 – 4.

In 1 Samuel 24 and 26 David had opportunities to kill Saul. But that would simply have created another kingdom of self-rule. That same attitude pervades 2 Samuel 1 – 4. In chapter 1 David does not celebrate the removal of his rival. He laments the fall of Israel's king. He does not reward the man who (supposedly) has killed Saul, but executes him for his regicide. In a mirror story in chapter 4, he again does not reward those who have killed his rival, but executes them for murder. He refuses to grasp the crown. In the midst of all the scheming, betrayals and violence of chapters 1 – 4, David entrusts himself to God.

Rekab and Baanah claim to be David's protectors because they have protected him from his enemies. They say, "Here is the head of Ish-Bosheth son of Saul, your enemy, who tried to kill you" (4:8). David begins his response with these words: "As surely as the LORD lives, who has delivered me out of every trouble" (4:9). In other words, *I don't need two men who kill people in their sleep to protect me. My protector is the LORD. And the LORD is not dead. He lives and it is he who delivers me from my enemies.*

Jesus—the ultimate Christ—also refused to seize power. In Luke 4 Satan came to him in the wilderness:

> "The devil led him up to a high place and showed him in an instant all the kingdoms of the world. And he said to him, 'I will give you all their authority and splendour; it has been given to me, and I can give it to anyone I want to. If you worship me, it will all be yours.'" (Luke 4:5-7)

It's an offer to fast-track the rise of Jesus to authority. Jesus can bypass the torment of the cross. But there is a price to pay, and that is the price of submission to Satan. As costly as the cross is, Jesus recognises that the cost of the alternative is higher for those he has come to save.

In the 1604 play *Doctor Faustus* by Christopher Marlowe (based on a German folk tale), Faustus is offered great powers in exchange for his soul. The play ends with Faustus being carried off to hell. It is a pact we make every time we choose expediency over morality—what suits us, or is the easiest thing to do, rather than what we know to be right. Jesus, however, refuses the offer—though it will cost him the cross. He entrusts himself to God. Quoting Deuteronomy 6:13, Jesus replies:

> "It is written: "Worship the Lord your God and serve him only."
>
> (Luke 4:8)

God will give Jesus a kingdom, and it will be an eternal kingdom which is free from compromise.

God vindicates David and he vindicates Jesus. This is how David understands what has happened. Through and despite the mess and brutality of power-politics, God has given him the kingdom:

- "He became more and more powerful, because the LORD God Almighty was with him" (**5:10**).

- "David knew that the LORD had established him as king over Israel and had exalted his kingdom for the sake of his people Israel (**5:12**).

- "The LORD ... chose me rather than your father or anyone from his house when he appointed me ruler over the LORD's people Israel" (6:21).

God makes David king. God has installed his anointed one. God will rule over humanity through his king. And even vicious scheming warlords like Abner can't stop it happening.

This is what happened at the resurrection and ascension of Jesus. Our attempt to get rid of God's rule reached its climax at the cross when we killed God's Messiah. But God raised him from the dead and Jesus ascended to heaven to receive all authority.

> Our attempt to get rid of God's rule reached its climax at the cross when we killed God's Messiah.

Jesus is not only our great example; he is also our Saviour. If he were just our example, then his example would crush us, for none of us are free from compromise. But the faithfulness of Jesus becomes our faithfulness if we are in Christ by faith. Through his obedience Jesus creates a new people of God.

Questions for reflection

1. Do you relate differently to the small and the great? How should our understanding of God's ways change our perspectives?

2. Psalm 2 shows us how God laughs in derision at those who oppose him. How will this help you as you meet those who mock God and sneer at his ways and those who follow him?

3. When we choose expediency over morality, we choose the way of Satan, not God. Where are you most tempted to compromise? Pray that you will be faithful to our faithful God today.

PART TWO

What is God Doing Today?

We, too, live in complicated times. Brute force and underhand betrayal are still part of life in this world. It's often hard to see what God is doing in our politics, in our culture, or indeed in our own lives. But we learn from the story of David that in the midst of this mess *the LORD will exalt the power of his christ*.

This is good news. The alternative is the **anarchy** of human selfishness and pride. God will establish his Son as the perfect, loving, godly King. Jesus the King brings justice and freedom to his people.

We see this in 2 Samuel 1 – 4. David brings peace. It's not perfect, for David is not the Christ; he's only a picture of God's ultimate King. But, when he's able to, he punishes injustice (1:15-16; 4:11-12). He establishes peace between Judah and Israel (3:21, 23). "All the people took note and were pleased; indeed, everything the king did pleased them" (3:36).

For many people the reign of God's King does not sound like good news. We would rather be in charge of our lives. We do not want God's King. But look at the mess we make of the world when left to ourselves. And look at God's king.

Our Husband: When all Israel enthrones David, they say, "We are your own flesh and blood" (**5:1**). It's literally "bone and flesh". It is an allusion to Genesis 2, when Adam first sees Eve and says she is "bone of my bone and flesh of my flesh". The implicit promise is that the king will husband the people—he will care for them as a husband cares for his wife. Ultimately, it's a picture of Jesus, the Husband who lays down his life for his bride (Ephesians 5:25-27).

Our Saviour: 2 Samuel **5:2** is literally "it was you who led out and brought in Israel" (ESV). This is military language. David led them into battle and led them home victorious. It's also a picture of Jesus, the Saviour who gives us victory over the enemies of sin and death.

Our Shepherd: The LORD says of David, "You shall shepherd my people Israel" (**v 2**). Again, it's a picture of Jesus, the Good Shepherd, who lays down his life for his sheep (John 10:11; see also Numbers 27:17; Ezekiel 34).

What is God doing today? God is working out his purposes and his chief purpose is to establish the reign of his Christ.

But what does that look like today? What is happening to the kingdom of Christ now?

In Revelation 2:26-27 Jesus quotes from Psalm 2. As we've seen, this is a royal psalm celebrating the rule of God's christ, possibly written to mark the enthronement of David. Jesus says:

"To the one who is victorious and does my will to the end, I will give authority over the nations— that one 'will rule them with an iron sceptre and will dash them to pieces like pottery'—just as I have received authority from my Father."

The Father Gives Authority to Jesus

In other words, Jesus is the Christ, David's great successor, God's anointed King. God has given Jesus authority over the nations. 2 Samuel 2:1-3 describes David's journey to Hebron to be crowned by Judah as an ascension: "David enquired of the LORD. 'Shall I go up …' The LORD said: 'Go up' … So David went up … ." David was anointed back in 1 Samuel 16. He then suffered for years on the margins before finally ascending to the throne. In the same way Jesus is anointed by the Holy Spirit at his baptism. He suffers for three years on the margins before ascending into heaven to receive all authority.

It is true that history is messy and it is true that it does not look as if Christ reigns. But the reason is that he has ascended to reign in heaven. And the reason he reigns in heaven—and not yet on earth—is to give people the chance to repent. It is not a sign of weakness. He is not cowering behind the gates of heaven in fear. Nor is it a dereliction of duty. He is being patient. When he comes to reign on earth—as he will—he will come to defeat rebels. But he is gracious and today he is giving people the opportunity to change sides before it is too late.

Jesus Gives Authority to Christians

"To him who is victorious … I will give authority over the nations" (Revelation 2:26). Jesus passes on the authority he has received to his people. Those who are victorious reign with the Christ. And those who are victorious extend the reign of the Christ. This poses a couple of a questions: Who are those "who are victorious"? And how do they reign with Christ?

Revelation 12:11 answers these questions: "They triumphed over [the devil] by the blood of the Lamb and by the word of their testimony; they did not love their lives so much as to shrink from death". Those who overcome and those who reign with Christ are those:

- who put their faith in the sacrificial death of Christ ("by the blood of the Lamb").

- who are involved in the mission of the church ("by the word of their testimony").

- who are willing to lay down their lives for Christ ("they did not love their lives so much as to shrink from death").

We do not reign with Christ with a sword. We reign through the word. We extend the kingdom of Christ as we proclaim the gospel to the nations. At the Great Commission Jesus said, "All authority in heaven and on earth has been given to me. Therefore go and make disciples of all nations, baptising them in the name of the Father and of the Son and of the Holy Spirit, and teaching them to obey everything I have commanded you. And surely I am with you always, to the very end of the age" (Matthew 28:18-20). It

> The reason Jesus reigns in heaven is to give people the chance to repent.

is because Jesus has become the Christ with all authority that we go to the nations. We command them to submit to the King. We extend the rule of God's Christ through the proclamation of the gospel.

Mission is messy. Life is messy. Often it is not clear what God is doing. But we can be confident of this: *The LORD will exalt the power of his Christ.*

This confidence enables us to endure hostility and take risks. Like David (in his best moments), we can maintain our integrity in the midst of power-politics, personal betrayal and missional setbacks because we know God will advance the kingdom of his Christ.

- Sometimes this confidence allows us to be passive. We will not take matters into our own hands. We will not compromise even when others take advantage of us. For we know that "it is not by strength that one prevails" (1 Samuel 2:9).

- Sometimes this confidence allows us to take risks. We do not fear failure because we know that God will advance his purposes. We do not fear adversity for we know "there is no Rock like our God" (1 Samuel 2:2).

When Paul first went to the city of Corinth, we are told that people opposed him and became abusive (Acts 18:6). Perhaps that is your experience. You have tried proclaiming Christ and people have been abusive. Maybe you feel like giving up. Maybe it feels like a waste of time. "One night the Lord spoke to Paul in a vision: 'Do not be afraid; keep on speaking, do not be silent. For I am with you, and no one is going to attack and harm you, because I have many people in this city'" (Acts 18:9-10). The LORD has many people in your town or city. *And the LORD will exalt the power of his Christ.*

Finally, what hope is there for rebels against God's King? Psalm 2 ends, "Blessed are all who take refuge in him" (Psalm 2:12). We're all rebels against God. We've all tried to live our lives without God. We all deserve his judgment. But Christ himself provides a refuge from his own judgment. He took the judgment that his people deserved on himself at the cross.

We get a hint of this in the 2 Samuel story. It appears just as an aside. 4:4 tells us that Saul has a crippled grandson Mephibosheth. At that time, when a king took power, he would often kill the entire family of his predecessor to

> Christ himself provides a refuge from his own judgment.

prevent any rival claims to the throne. We see this again and again in 1 and 2 Kings. So, when news of Saul's fall comes, Mephibosheth's nurse takes him and flees. She's terrified that Ish-Bosheth will have him killed. But as they flee, Mephibosheth falls and becomes disabled. We're probably told about Mephibosheth at this point to suggest that the only other option for the house of Saul is not viable. But the story also trails an important truth. Where will Mephibosheth be safe? The answer will be where we least expect it—*with David*. This "enemy" of David will find sanctuary in David's home (9:1-13). Where can you find refuge? When Christ returns to conquer humanity's rebellion, where will you be safe? The answer is: *in Christ*.

Questions for reflection

1. Jesus is our Husband. Think about this image, and reflect on its significance for us as his people. Jesus commits himself to us, and sacrificed himself willingly for us. We await a glorious future at the wedding feast of the Lamb. How will this change the way you think about the challenges you face today?

2. Jesus is our Saviour. He has rescued us from our enemies: death and judgment. How will this inform the way you think about yourself today?

3. Jesus is our Shepherd. He has not just done something for us in the past, and waits for it to be revealed in the future. He is our leader and guide day by day. How will this help you in any decision making you need to do today?

3. THE HOLINESS OF GOD

Someone was telling me recently how their grandmother loves **angels**. Her home is full of pictures of angels. What's that all about? I think the answer is that you get all the comfort of a divine reality without any of the demands. It is a way of domesticating God. The irony is that whenever angels appear in the Bible, they have the opposite effect to comfort—people are terrified!

Most people's view of God is that he is a kind of Father Christmas in the sky. It didn't use to be like this. The churches of medieval Europe were covered in murals depicting the final judgment in lurid detail. At best God appeared distant, someone at the top of the picture. At worst, he appeared cruel and vindictive. But in the last hundred years, perhaps uniquely in history, our culture has turned this on its head. Now we view God as benign, tame, indulgent. We have stripped him of his power. In a sense, we've handed over his power to the forces of nature, which continue to fill us with awe. And all that is left for our god to do is to forgive like an indulgent grandparent. But the true God—the God revealed in the Bible—is not tame.

In *The Lion, the Witch and the Wardrobe,* C. S. Lewis portrays Jesus as the Lion, Aslan. Early in the book Mr and Mrs Beaver describe him to the children. Mrs Beaver says, "If there's anyone who can appear before Aslan without their knees knocking, they're either braver than most or else just silly".

> God is dangerous. He's certainly not safe. But he is good.

So the children ask whether he's safe. Mr Beaver replies:

"Safe? ... Who said anything about safe? 'Course he isn't safe. *But he's good.*"

And that's what we see in 2 Samuel 5 – 6: God is dangerous. He's certainly not safe. But he is good.

God is Dangerous

Israel has been fighting a civil war and that suits their enemies, the Philistines. But now that war is over and David has been acclaimed king over all Israel. The Philistines are now threatened by a united Israel. So they seize the initiative and send a full force to find David (**5:17**). The phrase "to search for him" ominously recalls Saul's attempts to hunt down David in 1 Samuel. The Philistines spread out in "the Valley of Rephaim" (**v 18**). Rapha was a giant and the "Rephaim" are his descendants (21:16, 18, 20, 22). So this is the Valley of Giants and David will again be a giant-killer.

But the emphasis falls not on David, the slayer of giants, but on the LORD. David enquires of the LORD and the LORD promises to deliver the Philistines into his hands (**5:19**). There are really two battles. The first is described in **verse 20**:

"So David went to Baal Perazim, and there he defeated them. He said, 'As waters break out, the LORD has broken out against my enemies before me.' So that place was called Baal Perazim."

The LORD "breaks out" against the Philistines. So "the Philistines abandoned their idols there, and David and his men carried them off." (**v 21**). Back in 1 Samuel 4 the Philistines won a victory over Israel and carried off the ark of the covenant into the temple of their god, Dagon (1 Samuel 5:2). Now that is reversed. The Israelites defeat the Philistines and carry off their gods. The word for "abandoned" in

2 Samuel **5:21** is *azab* and the word for "idol" is *astab* so this is wordplay—a joke that highlights the impotent nature of idols. Their "gods" abandon them and so they are forced to abandon their gods. In 1 Samuel 31:9 the Philistines "sent messengers throughout the land of the Philistines to proclaim the news in the temple of their idols and among their people". Now those same idols are scattered across the battlefield.

The Philistines regroup for a second battle (2 Samuel **5:22**). David again enquires of God (**v 23**). This time God says:

"As soon as you hear the sound of marching in the tops of the balsam trees, move quickly, because that will mean the LORD has gone out in front of you to strike the Philistine army." (**v 24**)

The implication is that the sound of marching in the trees is the sound of the army of the LORD of hosts. The whooshing of leaves is the movement of God's angelic forces. It's akin to the moment at the end of *The Two Towers*, the second of the movies based on J. R. R. Tolkien's *The Lord of the Rings* trilogy. The orcs are fleeing the battle when they enter the forest of Fangorn. We see the tops of the trees swishing violently for a few moments and the orcs are heard of no more.

Back in 1 Samuel 8:20 the people asked for a king to "go out before us and fight our battles". Now the word "go out" is used to describe God. The sound of marching in the trees will be a sign that "the LORD has gone out in front of you to strike the Philistine army" (2 Samuel **5:24**). David clearly fights in **verses 20 and 25**. But the story is told to emphasise the actions of God. David enquires of God. God promises victory. God "breaks out" or "goes out". David is left to pick up the idols or pick off the stragglers.

The Philistines discover that God is dangerous. The living God fights for his people and all is well. Except that God's people are also about to discover that God is dangerous.

David decides it's time to bring the **ark of the covenant** to Jerusalem, his new capital city. The ark was a wooden chest covered in gold, containing the two tablets of stone that Moses brought down from

Mount Sinai, Aaron's rod and a sample of **manna**. It was a symbol of God's presence. This is how it's described in **6:2**:

> "the ark of God, which is called by the Name, the name of the LORD Almighty, who is enthroned between the **cherubim** on the ark."

First, we are told that the ark is called by "the Name". The Name of God represents God himself, particularly his character and his glory. Then, second, we're told that God is enthroned *between* the cherubim—a type of winged angel. The lid of the ark had carved cherubim on either side. So the ark was also a symbol of the throne or reign of God. It was the place where the throne of God met the earth.

There are two ark stories in Samuel with a number of similarities:

- The ark returns on a cart (1 Samuel 6:10-21; 2 Samuel **6:3**)

- God "struck down" Israelites (1 Samuel 6:19; 2 Samuel **6:7**)

- The ark resides temporarily (1 Samuel 7:1-2; 2 Samuel **6:10-11**)

- The ark is in "exile" in Gentile hands
  (1 Samuel 5:1-6:9; 2 Samuel **6:10-11**)

The key difference between the two stories is that in 1 Samuel the ark is *removed* from the **tabernacle** while in 2 Samuel it is *returned* to the tabernacle. In 1 Samuel 4:10 Saul lost 30,000 men. Now in 2 Samuel **6:1** 30,000 men accompany the ark home. In 5:6-16 David had conquered Jerusalem and this led to the establishment of his house in both senses of the word—a palace (5:11-12) and a family (5:13-14). Now in **5:17-25** God has won the victory, and chapter 6 is God's victory parade, leading to the establishment of his house. Just as God had "gone out in front" in battle (**5:24**), so now he goes out in front of the victory parade (**6:3-5**).

David and his men escort the ark on a cart to Jerusalem which great celebration (**v 1-5**). ("Baalah" in **verse 1** is another name for Kiriath Jearim, where the ark has resided for the last twenty years; see 1 Samuel 7:2.) Then disaster strikes. The oxen stumble. The cart jolts. The ark shifts. Uzzah reaches out his hand to stop it falling (**v 6**). And we read:

> "The LORD's anger burned against Uzzah because of his irreverent act; therefore God struck him down, and he died there beside the ark of God (**v 7**)."

> The ark was the place where the throne of God met the earth.

It's a shocking moment, and instinctively we sympathise with Uzzah. What should he have done? Should he have let the ark fall? How could God possibly blame someone, and punish them so fiercely, for a knee-jerk reaction like that?

But a deeper look reveals that Uzzah is not an innocent bystander. He is one of the men in charge of the operation (**v 3**). And this operation is not being conducted in the right way. It is a disaster waiting to happen. God had given the **Kohathites** the job of looking after the holy things like the ark. But it was a dangerous job. God warned:

> "the Kohathites must not go in to look at the holy things, even for a moment, or they will die" (Numbers 4:20).

So before the Kohathites could even think about moving the ark, the priests had to cover it first with a curtain, and then with a special leather case (Numbers 4:4-6, 17-20). There were six carts used in the work of the temple. But none of them were assigned to the Kohathites—no doubt to prevent this very scenario. Instead, the ark was only to be carried on their shoulders using poles (Numbers 7:6-9). Moreover, Israel had previous bitter experience of disrespectful dealings with the ark, which should have acted as a warning (1 Samuel 6:19-20). All this is ignored, and Uzzah suffers the consequences. This takes place at a threshing floor, which is often used as an image of judgment (Proverbs 20:26; see also 2 Samuel 24:16).

Perhaps we sympathise with Uzzah because we have not seen what the people of Beth Shemesh had seen after their earlier experience. They underestimated God's holiness and thought he was tame, and so ignored his instructions about the Ark, and were judged. They said:

"Who can stand in the presence of the LORD, this holy God?"

(1 Samuel 6:20)

God is Dangerous, Even to His People

2 Samuel **5:20** is literally:

"So David went to Baal Perazim [= Lord-Of-Outbreakings], and there he defeated them. He said, "As waters break out, the LORD has broken out against my enemies before me." So that place was called Baal Perazim [= Lord-Of-Outbreakings]."

Four times this verse uses the word for breaking out or outbreak. God broke out against the enemies of God's people. David likens it to waters breaking out. It's the image of a flash flood or dam bursting. Everything is carried away in a wave of destruction. **6:8** says literally:

"David was angry because the LORD's wrath had broken out against Uzzah, and to this day that place is called Perez Uzzah [= Outbreak-Against-Uzzah]."

It's the same language. Three times the same word is used: "broken out" or "outbreak". In both cases the outbreak of God is enshrined in the name of the place—Baal Perazim and Perez Uzzah. But this time God has broken out against his own people.

God is dangerous. He's dangerous to his enemies and he's dangerous to his people.

So David is afraid:

> God is a raging fire. If God comes to us, then we'll be consumed by the holy fire of his presence.

"David was afraid of the LORD that day and said, 'How can the ark of the LORD ever come to me?'" (**6:9**)

There is an answer to David's question. But we need to feel the full force of the question. *How can God ever come to us? How can God ever live with us?*

God is so holy that sin is burned up in his presence. And we're soaked in sin. We're like a rag doll soaked in the flammable liquid of our sin. And God is a raging fire. If God comes to us, then we'll be consumed by the holy fire of his presence.

We can't live with God because he is dangerous to sinners. But we can't live without him either, for God is the source of all good things.

Questions for reflection

1. "Safe? ... Who said anything about safe? 'Course he isn't safe. *But he's good.*" Does this description express how you think about God? Are you taking him seriously enough?

2. "God is not there for us. We are here for him." When is it easiest to forget this humbling truth?

3. David's great victories over the "old enemy", the Philistines are entirely down to God. How are you tempted to take the glory to yourself for victories—and lay the blame on God for failures?

PART TWO

God is Good

We can't live without God for God is good and the source of all that is good. The dangerous, terrifying ark, which brings curses and judgement with it, is left with Obed-Edom and the result is—blessing (**6:10-11**)! The ark that brought death is the same ark that now brings blessing.

A Gittite was someone from the Philistine city of **Gath**, and Obed-Edom means "servant of **Edom**". David has 600 Gittites from Gath in his army in 2 Samuel 15:18. So the man Obed-Edom is almost certainly a **Gentile**. The presence of the ark brings blessings, but it makes David jealous—perhaps seeking the blessing for Israel that is being enjoyed by a Gentile (**6:12**).

One of the great tensions of the Bible is this: you can't live with God, and you can't live without him. He's the holy God, who might break out against us because of our sin. But he's also the good God, who is the source of all that is good. When God eventually abandons his stubborn people in judgment upon them, the land is laid waste and the population is taken into exile. The message is clear. He is saying to them, *the food that you eat, the sun in the sky, the laughter you enjoy, the land in which you live—they all come from God.* And God's great intent for his people throughout the Bible story is not to destroy them, but to bless them with his presence.

So the good news is that there is an answer to the haunting question of **verse 9**: how can the presence of the LORD ever come to me? And we see a hint of it in the story.

David again brings the ark to Jerusalem and this time he succeeds. What's the difference? This time there's no mention of a cart. Instead people are carrying it (**v 12-13**). But there's another significant difference. "When those who were carrying the ark of the LORD had taken six steps, he sacrificed a bull and a fattened calf" (**v 13**). "They brought the ark of the LORD and set it in its place inside the tent that David had pitched for it, and David sacrificed burnt offerings and fellowship offerings before the LORD." (**v 17**) The journey begins and ends with sacrifice. (There's no mention of sacrifice in **verses 1-8.**) Not only that, but David is dressed in an **ephod**—and an ephod is a priestly garment (**v 14**; 1 Samuel 22:17-19).

What makes the difference? A "priest" offering a sacrifice. Something dies on route both times. The first time round it is Uzzah. The second time it is animals, dying in the place of the people. The first journey starts with celebration and ends in death and fear. The second starts with death—a sacrifice—but ends in blessing.

> The food that you eat, the sun in the sky, the laughter you enjoy, the land in which you live—they all come from God.

As the ark enters the city, David dances in a spontaneous expression of enthusiasm (2 Samuel **6:14-15**). People sometimes claim that David's uninhibited dancing is a mandate for dancing in the church today. Thankfully, they don't apply his example consistently and dance half-naked (**v 20**)! There are a few other examples of dancing in worship in the Old Testament (Exodus 15:20; Judges 21:19-20). They all appear to be spontaneous responses of joy rather than choreographed performances. Certainly David did not establish a dance troupe in the way he established a choir for the temple.

When the sacrifices were over, David...

"blessed the people in the name of the LORD Almighty. Then he gave a loaf of bread, a cake of dates and a cake of raisins to each person in the whole crowd of Israelites, both men and women."

(2 Samuel **6:18-19**)

God has come to his people and the people eat a meal in his presence. In every culture, eating a meal with someone is a sign of friendship and community. Eating a meal in the presence of God is the goal of the Bible story and the sign of our reconciliation with God.

> How can the presence of the Lord ever come to me? Through sacrifice.

So the answer to the question: *how can the presence of the* LORD *ever come to me?* is this: through sacrifice. And the sacrifices are a pointer to the blood of Jesus. At the cross God "broke out" against his own Son in our place so that we could come into his presence.

The language of God "breaking out" is also used at Mount Sinai: the people are not to touch the mountain or the LORD "will break out against them" (Exodus 19:20-24). But in Hebrews 12, reflecting on what Jesus has done, the writer pictures our experience of belonging to God's people by saying we do not come to Mount Sinai (Hebrews 12:18-21). We do not come to a mountain where God might break out against us. Instead we come to Mount Zion (Hebrews 12:22). Where is that? It's the mountain in Jerusalem where the ark ends up (2 Samuel 5:7; **6:16**).

David asks, "How can the ark of the LORD ever come to me?"(**v 9**) But it *does* come to Mount Zion. And now *we* can come to Mount Zion. Except we don't come to a literal mountain or a literal ark. The mountain and the box were both pointers to heaven and God himself (Hebrews 12:22-23). We come into the presence of God himself. How? Through "the sprinkled blood [of Jesus] that speaks a better word than the blood of **Abel**." (Hebrews 12:24) Abel was murdered and his blood cried out for vengeance. But the blood of Jesus cries out, "Mercy". It cries out, "Come".

But that doesn't mean we can now take God lightly. Hebrews goes on:

> "Let us be thankful, and so worship God acceptably with reverence and awe, for our 'God is a consuming fire.'"
>
> (Hebrews 12:28-29)

In the next chapter, Hebrews says we worship God with our lips and with our lives. So we're to live our whole lives in reverence and awe.

Living with the God Who is Dangerous and Good

What does it mean to live knowing that God is dangerous? We talk a lot about God's grace as if that trumps his holiness. And in one sense it does. If you put your faith in Jesus, then you don't need to fear God breaking out against you. But it's not that God used to be dangerous and now he's good. He is still holy. He's still a consuming fire. So what does it mean to live in reverence and awe?

There are some clues in the closing exchange in 2 Samuel 6. You couldn't make this up. One man stops the ark falling into the dust. Another man cavorts half-naked in a public worship ceremony. The first one is judged by God while the second is honoured by God!

But not by **Michal**. Michal is David's wife and Saul's daughter. In 1 Samuel 18:6-7 the women of Israel danced and sang as they rejoiced in David's victories. At that time Michal fell in love with David (v 20). Now there is more dancing and singing, but this time Michal despises David (2 Samuel **6:16, 20**). When he comes home, she confronts him.

1. Our Honour and God's Honour

First, Michal says, "How the king of Israel has distinguished himself today". She's being ironic. *You've not acted with the dignity or honour of a king*, she's saying. The word "distinguished" comes from the word "glory" or "weighty". *You've not given due weight to your position.*

Back in 1 Samuel 4:21-22 when the ark was taken away by the Philistines, **Phinehas'** wife said, "The Glory has departed". Michal and David use the same language now the ark has finally returned. Michal literally says, "How the king of Israel has glorified himself today. He has uncovered [or departed from his clothes] today in full view of the slave girls of his servants as any vulgar fellow would uncover or depart from himself." In effect she says, *the glory has departed because you took off your trousers.*

David responds, "I will become even more undignified than this, and I will be humiliated in my own eyes. But by these slave girls you spoke of, I will be held in honour" (2 Samuel **6:22**). In other words, *I'm not worried about my dignity or honour. In fact I'm willing to be humble, even humiliated for God's honour. Compared to the glory God, my glory doesn't matter.* Knowing that God is both dangerous and good means we worry more about God's honour than our honour.

Among the people of God such people are held in honour. By humiliating himself, David will be honoured by God's people. In his commentary on 2 Samuel, John Woodhouse entitles this section, "The joy of humility and the misery of pride". Jesus said, "Whoever wants to become great among you must be your servant" (Mark 10:43).

2. God's Opinion and Other People's Opinion

The second thing Michal says is this: you've been "going around half-naked in full view of the slave girls of his servants as any vulgar fellow would" (2 Samuel **6:20**). Not just in view of his servants, but in view of "the slave girls of his servants". These are the lowest of the low in the eyes of a snob. What matters to Michal is how people view you.

David responds:

"It was before the LORD, who chose me rather than your father or anyone from his house when he appointed me ruler over the LORD's people Israel—I will celebrate before the LORD." (**v 21**)

In other words, *The only audience that really matters to me is God. I wasn't celebrating before the slave girls. I don't care what they think about me. I was celebrating before God.*

"In full view" of the slave girls in **verse 20** is literally "in the eyes of"—a phrase David repeats in **verse 22** to speak of himself. It highlights the key issue: whose view of you matters, and what do they see?

- In the eyes of Michal, David is dishonoured because of his humility (**v 20**).

- In the eyes of David himself, David is humiliated (**v 22**).

- In the eyes of God's people, David is honoured because of his humility (**v 22**).

- In the eyes of God, David is chosen for honour above Saul's family (**v 21**; 7:19).

"I am more surprised at David dancing than fighting," said Pope Gregory the Great: "For by fighting he subdued his enemies; but by dancing before the Lord he overcame himself" (*Morals on the Book of Job* 27.46).

Our greatest struggles are with ourselves, with our own pride and selfishness. How does David overcome his pride? By focusing on God rather than himself, and by focusing on God's opinion rather than the opinion of other people. For David, it is God's view of him that matters, and he knows how God views him for God has chosen him as ruler over God's people (**6:21**). Saul worried about what people thought of him (1 Samuel 15:30) and as a result he has been despised throughout history. David is happy to be despised for God's sake and as a result he is honoured among God's people (2 Samuel **6:22**).

> Our greatest struggles are with ourselves, with our own pride and selfishness.

It's not that God chose David because he was humble. It's the other way round. David can rise above the opinion of other people because he knows he is chosen by God. It's precisely the same for us. We rise above the opinion of others to the extent that we believe ourselves to be God's chosen children. David is not literally naked—he has removed his royal clothes. In other words, he's not hiding behind his position. He doesn't fear exposure because he's confident that God views him with favour.

David's response to Michal is to remind her that God chose him over her father's family. That choice is confirmed in God's judgment on Michal. "And Michal daughter of Saul had no children to the day of her death" (**v 23**). The text highlights that she is Saul's daughter to show that the house of Saul has no future.

You may be circling round the edges of the church. You like what you see. But you hesitate to commit yourself. You don't want to make the jump. Perhaps you worry what others will say. Perhaps you worry about losing control of your life. Remember: *God is dangerous*. The Bible says, "You are storing up wrath against yourself for the day of God's wrath" when God will break out against you and there will be no place to hide (Romans 2:5).

> Our watchwords must be, "I will be humiliated in my own eyes", and, "I will celebrate before the Lord".

Or perhaps you're a Christian, but you feel stuck. Maybe you're stuck in some sin. Maybe you have plateaued and you can't make progress. It might be because you're more worried about your reputation than God's glory. You cling to the idea that you can overcome sin yourself because you don't want to be humiliated in your own eyes. Maybe you won't ask for help because you can't admit you struggle.

Or maybe you've seen other Christians expressing their emotions in public—crying during a sermon or jigging with joy during a song—and you despise them. "How undignified." "In full view of other people." I've thought those thoughts. We're like Michal in the story. And then we wonder why our spiritual lives are barren.

Or perhaps you hesitate to tell people about Jesus because you're worried about what they'll think of you. The opinion of people matters more to you than the opinion of God—the God who is dangerous and good.

Or maybe your heart is divided because you cling to some sin. You think it doesn't matter because God will indulge you. You can't let go of your sin because you think life without it would feel empty. But God is dangerous. And God is good. He doesn't offer us a lesser life. He offers us a full life and a rich life.

Our watchwords must be, "I will be humiliated in my own eyes" (2 Samuel **6:22**), and, "I will celebrate before the LORD" (**v 21**).

Questions for reflection

1. "Our greatest struggles are with ourselves, with our own pride and selfishness." How far do you think this is true of yourself? How are you dealing with it?

2. How influenced are you by the opinions of others? How can you help yourself focus more on God's opinion of you?

3. "I will celebrate before the LORD." Sometimes this happens spontaneously, but at other times, we must force ourselves to reflect on his goodness and mercy, so that our worship of God is stimulated. How will you encourage yourself to celebrate God's goodness to you this week?

4. A KING FOR ALL HUMANITY

Not only is 2 Samuel 7 the most important chapter in 1 and 2 Samuel, it's one of the most important chapters in the entire Bible. Yet, after all the dramatic twists and turns of the opening chapters of 2 Samuel, it can feel as if not much happens. All the "action" is in the form of conversations. But this chapter is, as it were, a vital structural span on the bridge linking the *promise* of a Saviour to Adam with the *coming* of the Saviour in Jesus. So what happens in this chapter is alluded to, either explicitly or implicitly, all over the pages of the Bible. The words spoken by God in this chapter are still shaping human history today.

Verse 1 says "The LORD had given [David] rest from all his enemies around him". On the seventh day of creation God rested (Genesis 2:1-3). This is the only day of creation without a version of the formula: "and there was evening, and there was morning—the first day" (Genesis 1:5, 8, 13, 19, 23, 31). It suggests that this **Sabbath** is a day without end, an eternal rest in which humanity is invited to share (Hebrews 4:1-6).

But humanity rejected God's invitation and instead was cursed with rest-less labour (Genesis 3:17-19) and peace-less conflict. But God graciously promised rest to his people—a promise marked by each Sabbath day. Joshua fulfilled this promise in the conquest of the land (Joshua 21:43-45)—it became a place of rest for the wandering and homeless people of God. But this fulfilment was only partial. The people didn't fully trust God, so they lacked the confidence to completely drive out the inhabitants of the land (Judges 2:1-3). From that time on the nations around Israel were a thorn in her side, disturbing their peace. Only now under the reign of David, God's anointed king, can the people enjoy rest from their enemies (as chapter 8 will elaborate).

The peace brought by David, however, will prove to be short-lived. David's own sin will bring conflict right to the heart of the nation (as we'll see in 2 Samuel 11 – 20). But this moment is a picture of the rest Jesus brings. For Jesus defeats the ultimate enemies of God's people—sin and death—so we can share in God's *eternal* Sabbath. When Jesus says, "Come to me, all you who are weary and burdened, and I will give you rest", he's claiming to be God's Messiah, come to defeat our enemies and establish God's kingdom (Matthew 11:28).

In the meantime, with peace established, David's thoughts go to the construction of a temple for God (2 Samuel **7:2**). David wants to house the ark that's now in Jerusalem (6:16). There's perhaps even a hint of embarrassment in the contrast between David's beautiful cedar palace and God's travel-worn tent (**7:2**).

In Deuteronomy 12:10-11 Moses had warned the people not to worship God according to the ways of the nations. They were to centralise worship in a temple so it could be properly regulated. The trigger for this was when God had given them rest from their enemies—the very situation that now pertained. So David's instinct is a good one and initially commended by the prophet Nathan (2 Samuel **7:3**).

But God has other ideas (**v 4**). God himself had sanctioned a temple and will bless the temple built by David's son. So why does God postpone at this point? The answer seems to be that God wants to highlight two key truths.

A Provision from God Not David

The key words in **verse 5** are "you" and "me". "Are *you* the one to build *me* a house?" God does not need David. It's not as if God has ever needed a house (**v 6**) or been lobbying for one (**v 7**). The king may have a palace, but God lives among his people. When the temple is finally built, Solomon wisely acknowledges that "the heavens, even the highest heaven, cannot contain you. How much less this temple I have built!" (1 Kings 8:27; see also Acts 7:48-49).

Indeed, it's God who has provided for David (2 Samuel **7:8-11**). Having asked, "Are you the one to build me a house?" God now flips the pronouns in **verses 8-9**. David's perspective is turned on its head. David's focus has been on what he might do for God. But what really matters is what God has done for David: "I took you ... I have been with you ... I have cut off all your enemies ... I will make your name great" (**v 8-9**). This echoes the language of Genesis 12:2. In Genesis 11:4 people vainly try to

> Only when God's King has defeated the last enemy, death itself, can God's people enjoy the eternal Sabbath of God.

make a name for themselves. By contrast God promises Abraham, "I will make your name great". This allusion back to Abraham is a clue that the promise to Abraham is about to be focused on and fulfilled by Israel's king.

In 2 Samuel **7:10-11** God moves out beyond David to Israel as a nation. David had assumed he would build a home for God. But the reality is that God is creating a home for his people (**v 10**). He will complete the unfinished task of defeating the enemies of his people so they can enjoy rest (**v 11**). The "rest" described in **verse 11** echoes the "rest" described in **verse 1**. But here it's a *future promise* rather than a *present reality*. The rest enjoyed by David would prove fleeting. Only when God's King has defeated the last enemy, death itself, can God's people enjoy the eternal Sabbath of God.

The language and the promises all emphasise God's power. As Paul says in Athens:

"The God who made the world and everything in it is the Lord of heaven and earth and does not live in temples built by human hands. And he is not served by human hands, as if he needed anything." (Acts 17:24-25)

The narrator describes David as "the king" (2 Samuel **7:1, 3**). But God calls him "my servant" (**v 5**).

Yet this episode also highlights God's grace. There are many examples of ancient Near-Eastern kings "paying" for the blessing of their deity through the construction of a temple in a kind of *quid pro quo* contract—I build you a magnificent temple; you enable me to live long, prosper and defeat my enemies. But these kinds of quid pro quo relationships are not how it works with our God. David gets status, wealth, victory and glory without payment. Indeed, God gently reminds David that he was once just a shepherd boy (**v 8**). Everything David has, he has from God.

The reason why David will not build the temple is to prevent any suggestion that God depends on human assistance. It's we humans who are utterly dependent on God.

A House for David Not a House for God

David proposed to build a house for God in the sense of a temple. God's counterproposal is to build a house for David in the sense of a **dynasty**. "Are you the one to build me a house?" (**v 5**) is answered in **verse 11**: No, "the LORD himself will establish a house for you".

Verses 12-13 have Solomon in view, David's son by **Bathsheba**. Solomon is the one who will succeed David (**v 12**, see also 1 Chronicles 22:7-10) and it's Solomon who will eventually build the temple (**v 13**). But **verses 14-16** push this far beyond the immediate succession in three ways.

First, the word "offspring" or "seed" in **verse 12** is another *echo of the promise to Abraham* (Genesis 12:7). The Bible plays on the ambiguity of this word. Is it singular or plural? It's clearly plural in Genesis 13:15-16, which says that Abraham's offspring will be so numerous they can't be counted. Yet Paul says it's singular (Galatians 3:16).

This is a promise of *one particular offspring*—Jesus Christ. The point of this double meaning is that Christ is the promised Saviour, but through him God will save a great multitude. Abraham's offspring is both singular and many: Christ and his people. One representative will redeem God's people as a whole. What God promises now to David is that the Rescuer will be from David's line. So this promise is not just a promise of **succession**. It's a promise of salvation.

Second, *God promises to be a father to David's son*. "I will be his father, and he shall be my son" (2 Samuel **7:14**). In Exodus 4:22-23 God described Israel as "my son". Now the same language is applied to the king. The Davidic king is going to be the **personification** of the nation. At a practical level, throughout Israel's history the people would follow the king's lead. So the fidelity of the king is the key factor shaping the fidelity (or otherwise) of the nation. But more than this, the king is the *representative* of the nation. His actions determine the fate of the nation. Most of the time this will mean his sin led to judgment on the nation (2 Samuel **7:14**). But at one key moment the obedience of David's greatest son, the Lord Jesus, will save God's people. As our representative, his righteousness becomes our righteousness.

Third, *God promises an eternal kingdom* (**v 13, 16**). David had replaced Saul as king so Saul hadn't been succeeded by his heir (**v 15**). No Saulite dynasty had formed. But God draws a sharp contrast between Saul and David. Saul's dynasty was cut short. David's dynasty will be eternal. "Your house and your kingdom shall endure for ever before me; your throne shall be established for ever" (**v 16**). Throughout the centuries that followed, God kept that promise. The nation divided into ten northern tribes (known as "Israel") and two southern tribes (known as "Judah'). In the northern kingdom of Israel military **coup** followed military coup. Only rarely did dynasties form—and then not for long; usually ended by murder or death in battle. But through all the chaos of Judah's history, the king was *always* a "son of David"—not through any personal merit, but because of God's promise (1 Kings 15:3-4). Sin could not confound

God's purposes. Individual kings might be condemned (2 Samuel **7:14**), but the line would always continue. The dynastic line continued beyond the **exile**, despite the king being deposed. Finally the angel Gabriel announced to Mary:

> "You will conceive and give birth to a son, and you are to call him Jesus. He will be great and will be called the Son of the Most High. The Lord God will give him the throne of his father David, and he will reign over Jacob's descendants for ever; his kingdom will never end." (Luke 1:31-33)

It's full of echoes of 2 Samuel 7. "He will be great" fulfils **verse 9**; "the Son of the Most High" fulfils **verse 14**; and a throne that never ends fulfils **verse 16**. Both the adoptive father and human mother of Jesus are from the line of David. When the voice from heaven says, "You are my Son" (Mark 1:11; 9:7) or when Peter confesses Jesus to be "the Messiah, the Son of the living God" (Matthew 16:16), they have in mind 2 Samuel **7:14**. In view is not primarily the *divine* sonship of Jesus (though, of course, the Bible affirms this in many other places), but the *Davidic* sonship of Jesus.

> Jesus is not just another king in the line of David. He is its ultimate destination.

But Jesus is not just another king in the line of David. He is its *ultimate destination*. He is, as a well-known hymn puts it, "great David's greater Son". He will be the King who ultimately rescues God's people and reigns over them for ever. At the cross it looked as if the Davidic line had finally been extinguished. But God raised Jesus from the dead. And in doing so, says Peter, "God has made this Jesus, whom you crucified, both Lord and Messiah" (Acts 2:36). Now Jesus has ascended to receive the eternal throne promised to the house of David.

"If you tell me 2 Samuel 7 is just about Solomon", the early church father Tertullian said, "you will send me into a fit of laughter".

"Because Christ rather than any other was to build the temple of God, that is to say, a holy manhood, wherein God's Spirit might dwell as in a better temple, Christ rather than David's son Solomon was to be looked for as the Son of God."

(*Against Marcion* 3.20)

Why didn't God allow David to build a temple? Perhaps because his was a kingship won through battle and blood (1 Chronicles 21:8). Perhaps also because David *assumed* it would be his crowning achievement and the culmination of "Project-David". **Verse 1** certainly has that feel about it. David is "settled". His rule is established. He has rest from his enemies. All that's left is to build a temple for God. John Woodhouse says:

"The Lord seems to suggest that David's motivation for thinking about building this house arose from a sense of having arrived … However, the Lord was not yet ready to rest from his work on behalf of his people or from the fulfilment of his promise to Abraham." (*2 Samuel: Your Kingdom Come*, page 213)

God has much bigger plans for "Project-David"—plans that will culminate only when we see the salvation of a new humanity and rest in a new creation. The work of the Davidic dynasty has only just begun. This is why this chapter is so important in the plotline of the Bible.

We'll see how we are to respond to God's big "Project-David" in **verses 18-29**. For now, let's join Peter in saying to Jesus, "You are the Messiah, the Son of the living God" (Matthew 16:16). This is the key response to David's greatest Son: to recognise his rule and entrust ourselves to his care.

Questions for reflection

1. Reflect on the faithfulness of God to his promises to Abraham and to David. They were tested through sin, **apostasy** and the constant and repeated unfaithfulness of God's people. How does this encourage you in regard to God's promises to you in Christ?

2. Do you ever default to a quid pro quo approach to relationship with God? Why is that so wrong? How can we help ourselves relate to God through grace?

3. Jesus is your eternal ruler, shepherd, defender and provider. What will it mean to entrust yourself to his care...

PART TWO

No Give, All Take

In 2 Samuel **7:11-16** God makes a covenant with David, promising him an eternal dynasty. This word came to the prophet Nathan (**v 4**), who faithfully reported it to David (**v 17**). As a result David "went in and sat before the LORD." The rest of chapter consists of David's words to God in response to God's words to David.

David and Humanity

David thought building the temple would round off God's amazing work in his life. David already knew that God had established him as king (5:12). He thought that being settled in his palace and enjoying rest from his enemies (**7:1**) was an amazing act of divine generosity. "And yet this was a small thing in your eyes, O LORD God" (**v 19** ESV). He was just beginning to realise that God had much bigger plans for David's house. "This ... small thing" in **verse 19** (ESV) is contrasted with "this great thing" in **verse 21**.

So David continues, "This decree, Sovereign LORD, is for the human race" (NIV footnote). Or, "This is instruction for mankind, O LORD God!" (ESV). It's literally *torah ha'adam*: **torah** or law or covenant for Adam. The word "Adam" is the name of the first man, but also a term for humanity as a whole because Adam was the representative of humanity.

> "This brief exclamation expresses David's far-reaching under-standing of the promise he had heard."
> (John Woodhouse, *2 Samuel: Your Kingdom Come*, page 225)

God dealt with humanity in Adam (as Paul explains in Romans 5:12-21). What Adam did, he did on our behalf. And God's verdict on Adam is his verdict on us all. When Adam fell, God promised a new Adam through whom he would restore humanity. In the promises to Abraham, God focused his saving purposes on Israel. Israel would be the nation through whom God saved humanity. With the covenant with David, God's saving purposes were now focused on the king.

So the focus of God's purpose moves *from humanity to Israel to the king*. But always the intent is to move back in the other direction. The king brings blessing to Israel, which brings blessing to humanity. The king is the son of God, who will redeem Israel the son of God, who will redeem the race of Adam the son of God (2 Samuel **7:14**; Exodus 4:22-23; Luke 3:38).

So God will deal with humanity through his king. The king becomes our representative. The future of humanity is linked to the future of David's house. This covenant is how God will save humanity. God is making a contract to adopt humanity through David's son. Those in the Christ will be God's sons just as the Christ is God's Son. So this covenant with David is actually a covenant with humanity.

In 2 Corinthians 6:14-7:1 Paul quotes the covenant with David: "As God has said ... And "I will be a Father to you, and you will be my sons and daughters," says the Lord Almighty". Not only does Paul apply the covenant with David to the church in Corinth; he also changes the original quotation. He transforms the reference to a son (singular) into a reference to sons (plural) and adds a reference to daughters. He changes the promise that the king will be God's son (singular) into a promise that God will adopt many sons and daughters. The promise for the king quite explicitly becomes a promise for all God's people. It becomes a promise for us through the original and primary focus of the promise: Jesus Christ. Jesus is the true representative and the true Son. He is the true Adam, the true Israel and the true David.

So we can see David's response to God's covenant as a model for our response. In verses 2 Samuel **7:18-24** David responds in *praise* for what God has done in the past (corresponding to God's words in **v 5-11**), and then in **verses 25-29** he responds in *prayer* for what God has promised to do in the future (corresponding to God's words in **v 11-16**). We can detect in the stillness of his posture (**v 18**), the rhetorical questions (**v 19, 23**) and the struggle for words (**v 20**) something of the deep sense amazement felt by David.

The Promise That Leads to Praise

David addresses God as "Sovereign LORD". It's a phrase that occurs in the books of Samuel only in this prayer. It's also a phrase Abraham uses only in response to God's promise (Genesis 15:2, 8). The phrase combines *Adonai* (the general Hebrew word for a "lord" or "master") with *Yahweh* (the special name of God which is usually indicated in our Bibles by "LORD" in capital letters). So David says, "my Lord LORD" or "my master LORD". It's the counterpart to God's description of "my servant David" (2 Samuel **7:5, 8**). Indeed, ten times in this prayer David refers to himself as "your servant".

God has done a gracious thing. "For you know your servant" in **verse 20** is probably David's recognition of his sin and inadequacy. *You know want I'm really like*, David is admitting. God's promises are not based on David's merit, but "according to your will" (**v 21**, literally "your heart"). "What more can David say to you?" (**v 20**) Clearly David does have more to say—otherwise we wouldn't have **verses 21-29** in our Bibles. But no words can adequately express the praise due to God for his grace.

God has done a great thing. David describes the covenant as a "great thing", far surpassing his expectations (**v 21**). And the "great thing" of **verse 21** leads inevitably to the conclusion in **verse 22**, "How great you are". The acts of God reveal the character of God—and God is beyond compare (**v 22**; 1 Samuel 2:2).

David then extends out from himself to the nation as a whole. The question: "Who am I?" in 2 Samuel **7:18** becomes, "Who is like your people Israel?" in **verse 23**. And the uniqueness of God in **verse 22** leads to the uniqueness of his people in **verse 23**: "And who is like your people Israel?" What makes God's people so special? They are "the one nation on earth that God went out to redeem as a people for himself" (**v 23**). What makes the church special? We are the only group on earth who have been redeemed from sin and death to enjoy a relationship with God. Not only that, but the eternal reign of God's King (**v 13, 16**) will create an eternal relationship for God's people with God (**v 24**).

But the emphasis here is not on the people, but on God. God has done this "to make a name for himself" (**v 23**). Any talk of the privileges of being part of God's people must lead us back to our God in praise.

The Promise That Leads to Prayer

In **verse 25** David turns to prayer. And his prayer is perhaps somewhat surprising. David asks God to do what God has already said he will do: "And now, LORD God, keep for ever the promise you have made concerning your servant and his house. Do as you promised." This may seem strange, but the pattern of asking God to do what God has already promised is repeated again and again in Bible prayers.

- Moses pleads for mercy for Israel after the golden-calf incident by asking God to remember his promise to Abraham (Exodus 32:12-13).

- **Nehemiah** prays for struggling Jerusalem by asking God to remember his promise to Moses (Nehemiah 1:8-9).

- In Nehemiah 9:7-8 the people pray on the basis of God's promise to Abraham.

- Daniel asks God to deliver the Jews after 70 years in exile after reading Jeremiah's promise that God would deliver the Jews after 70 years (Daniel 9:1-3).

The **Puritan** William Gurnall said, "Prayer is nothing but the promise reversed or God's word turned inside out and formed into an argument and retorted back again upon God by faith".

It's not just that we can pray using God's promises. Praying God's promises also gives us *confidence* in prayer. In 2 Samuel **7:27** David says, "LORD Almighty, God of Israel, you have revealed this to your servant, saying, 'I will build a house for you.' So your servant has found courage to pray this prayer to you." What can we poor, feeble sinners presume to ask of the Sovereign Creator? The answer is: *what he has promised to give us*. Another Puritan, John Trapp, said:

> "Promises must be prayed over. God loves to be burdened with and to be urgently pressed with requests in his own words. He loves to even be sued upon his own bond. For prayer is putting God's promises into suit. And it is no arrogancy nor presump-tion to burden God, as it were, with his own promises."
> (John Trapp, *A Commentary on the Old and New Testaments*)

1 John 5:14 says, "This is the confidence we have in approaching God: that if we ask anything according to his will, he hears us". But how do we know what God's will is? Not through some mysterious process or inner voices. We know God's will because he's told us in his word. We can be confident that we're making appropriate requests when they align with God's promises. "Does this mean I can't pray for my sick child?" you might ask. "After all, I have no specific promise that my child will get better." Yes, you can pray of your child to be healed. God has promised to hear our prayers with compassion. But God's promises should shape *the way* you pray. Your prayer should be shaped by a concern for God's glory and the advance of the kingdom promised to David.

> We can be confident that we're making appropriate requests when they align with God's promises.

We have a model for praying on the basis of God's covenant prom-ises to David in Psalm 89.

> "I will sing of the steadfast love of the Lord, forever;
> with my mouth I will make known your
> faithfulness to all generations.

For I said, 'Steadfast love will be built up forever;
> in the heavens you will establish your faithfulness.'
You have said, 'I have made a covenant with my chosen one;
> I have sworn to David my servant:
"I will establish your offspring forever,
> and build your throne for all generations'". (Psalm 89:1-4, ESV)

The psalmist sets the covenant with David (v 1-4) alongside God's council with the angels (v 5-8) and his defeat of chaos at creation (v 9-13). The covenant with David is as significant as the act of creation. Why? Because it's a key stepping-stone in the story of re-creation.

And yet to the psalmist it feels as if God has "renounced the covenant with your servant" (v 38-39). The foes of God's people are exalted (v 42) and the Davidic king is scorned (v 41, 50-51). It could be a description of our generation, in which the church suffers and the name of Jesus is mocked. So, on the basis of God's covenant promise to David, we can and should cry out with the psalmist, "How long, LORD?"

But there is hope. The psalmist doubts neither God's ability nor his commitment: "Your arm is endowed with power; your hand is strong, your right hand exalted. Righteousness and justice are the foundation of your throne; love and faithfulness go before you" (v 13-14). There's also a hint of what's to come in his description of the Davidic king: "You have cut short the days of his youth; you have covered him with a mantle of shame" (v 45). One day the King would die on a cross in shame. And it would seem as if the promise has floundered. But on the third day Jesus will rise again. His death would be the means by which God defeats the final enemy. And his resurrection would be the promise of eternal vindication.

The Glory of God Among the Nations

God's promise is not the only "argument" David uses with God. He also invites God to consider his glory. "Do as you promised, so that your name will be great for ever. Then people will say, 'The LORD Almighty is God over Israel!'" (2 Samuel **7:25-26**) Again this is a common concern for Bible pray-ers.

- When God threatened to destroy Israel after she had refused to enter the promised land, Moses prayed on the basis of God's reputation. He boldly suggested that the Egyptians would conclude God was unable to protect his people if the people were destroyed (Numbers 14:13-16).

- When Jerusalem was threatened by the Assyrians, **Hezekiah** prayed for deliverance "so that all kingdoms of the earth may know that you, LORD, are the only God" (Isaiah 37:20).

- **Daniel** asked God to deliver the exiles "for your sake ... because your city and your people bear your Name" (Daniel 9:17-19).

- The glory of God dominates many of Paul's prayers (Romans 15:5-6; Ephesians 3:20-21; Philippians 1:11; 2 Thessalonians 1:12).

2 Samuel **7:28-29** sums up David's prayer. On the basis of God's covenant faithfulness (**v 28**), he prays for blessing: "Now be pleased to bless the house of your servant, that it may continue for ever in your sight; for you, Sovereign LORD, have spoken, and with your blessing the house of your servant will be blessed for ever".

The threefold reference to blessing again echoes God's promise to Abraham in Genesis 12:2-3. The covenant with David is the latest act in the fulfilment of that promise. And the promise to Abraham included the promise that "all peoples on earth will be blessed through you". Just as God's covenant with Abraham is a blessing for "all peoples", so God's covenant with David is *torah* for all humanity. Today this blessing is reaching the nations through the mission of the church. And this must be a central theme of our prayers. Because of this promise, and on the basis of this promise, we pray for mission.

Questions for reflection

1. Do you find it harder to praise God than to ask him for things? Why is that? And how can we cultivate a habit and attitude of praise?

2. What promises from God to you as a Christian can you directly turn into prayers?

3. How will a hunger for the glory of God turn into a desire to reach out with the gospel to others—and to pray for those who do that?

5. LIKE A SON

In 2 Samuel 7 God makes a covenant with King David. He promises

- "I will make your name great" (7:9).

- "I will provide a place for my people" (7:10).

- "I will … give you rest from all your enemies" (7:11).

Not only will God do this *now*. He will do it *for ever*. He will establish the house or the dynasty of David for ever (7:11-16). One of David's sons will reign over God's people for ever. "I will be his father, and he shall be my son" (7:14). David says this is *torah adam*: "law for humanity". This is how God will save the world.

Psalm 2 quotes from 2 Samuel 7, and shows how God's promise has a worldwide impact in view. The psalm is a great commentary on what happens next in 2 Samuel 8 – 10. But, as we saw when we looked at 2 Samuel 5, Psalm 2 also looks forward to the *ultimate* Christ. It is one of the most frequently quoted psalms in the New Testament. The apostles saw Psalm 2 (and therefore also passages like 2 Samuel 8 – 10) as prophetic for, and a commentary on, the reign of Jesus

The psalm begins with the kings of the earth rebelling against God and his anointed king, his christ (2:1-3). But God responds by affirming his commitment to establish his king (2:4-6). And the christ responds by quoting God's covenant: "He said to me, 'You are my son; today I have become your father'" (2:7). And then God says to the king:

"Ask me,

and I will make the nations your inheritance,

the ends of the earth your possession.

You will rule them with a rod of iron;

you will dash them to pieces like pottery." (Psalm 2:8-9)

This is the pattern that unfolds in 2 Samuel 8.

The Ends of the Earth Belong to the Christ

"In the course of time" in **verse 1** is not **chronological** but **thematic**. Chapter 8 brings together events from across David's reign to demonstrate the truth of 2 Samuel 7:9, that God has cut off all David's enemies.

- David defeats and subdues the Philistines (**8:1**).

- David defeats the **Moabites**, executing two-thirds of their army (**v 2**).

- David defeats and subdues the **Arameans** (**Zobah** in **verse 3** and **Damascus** in **verse 5** were both Aramean cities), **hamstringing** their chariot horses in **verse 4** because Israel didn't use chariots (see Psalm 20:7).

- David defeats and subdues the Edomites (2 Samuel **8:13-14**).

Some of David's actions seem brutal and merciless (**v 2**). If you feel a sense of abhorrence at this, and other things done in war "in the name of God", don't worry—it is right to feel this way. God himself takes no pleasure in the death of the wicked (Ezekiel 18:23), and neither should we. But we must not judge the practices and actions of ancient warriors by modern standards of warfare. They were very different times, and, strange as it may seem to us, this mass execution of the defeated army may actually have seemed like a kindness to the first readers of 2 Samuel, and perhaps even to the nations surrounding Israel. Many other countries were far more brutal in their torture and treatment of defeated prisoners after a battle.

But this is not a mandate for **genocide** or war crimes either. Moab's sins were long-standing. They had been persistent enemies of God's people, and worshipped cruel gods. Child sacrifice and prostitution were common. David was acting as God's agent in bringing a just judgment upon them. David is repeatedly said to "strike down" his enemies (translated in the NIV as "defeated" in **8:1, 2, 3, 9**; "struck" or "subdued" in **verses 5 and 11**; and "victory over" in **verse 10**). It's the word used of God striking down the Philistines in 5:24-25 and Uzzah in 6:7. Those who reject David's rule are not just rejecting a human king, but the living God himself. This is the message of Psalm 2. David is the agent of *divine judgment*. By all means let's ask our honest questions of the text of Scripture, but we must be careful not to stand in judgment over

> We must not judge the practices and actions of ancient warriors by modern standards of warfare.

the Bible. We must let the word of God judge our attitudes. It is easy for us to understand God's judgment on some people whom we consider exceptionally evil—murderers, child molesters, etc. But we find it more difficult to understand how God might judge our "nice" kind neighbour. But the reality is that *all humanity* faces God's judgment. The surprise is that God graciously spares anyone at all. The surprise was that David lets a third of the Moabites go free.

2 Samuel 8 describes victories to the west (**v 1**), east (**v 2**), north (**verses 3-5**) and south (**v 13-18**). David rules the four corners of his world. Between the two descriptions of conquest (**v 1-6, 13-14**) is an account of **plunder** and **tribute** (**v 7-10**). The plunder belongs to the victor. But in David's case the true victor is God so David dedicates the plunder to God (**v 11-12**; see Revelation 21:24, 26). The narrative focuses on David's battle against Hadadezer. "Hadadezer" means "Hadad is a help", and Hadad was another name for Baal, the Canaanite sky-god. In 1 Samuel 7:12 Samuel raised a stone, naming it Ebenezer, "Stone of Help", as a reminder that "thus far the Lord has helped us". In contrast the god Hadad is no help at all. So Hadadezer

is forced to turn to his fellow Arameans, but they are no help either—not against the LORD and his christ.

Key to the writer's intent are the two summary statements that conclude the two accounts of conquest: "The LORD gave David victory wherever he went" (2 Samuel **8: 6, 14**). This is the fulfilment of the promise of Psalm 2:8: "I will make the nations your inheritance, the ends of the earth your possession". The nations belong to the christ.

2 Samuel **8:13** literally says, "David made a name for himself" (ESV). But we should not interpret this as self-aggrandisement. It's a summary statement of the truth that God made a name for David by giving him victory. It's a fulfilment of God's promise in 7:9: "Now I will make your name great, like the names of the greatest men on earth".

But chapter 8 is not just about David. The result for God's people is peace. It is a fulfilment of the covenant promise of 7:10: "And I will provide a place for my people Israel and will plant them so that they can have a home of their own and no longer be disturbed. Wicked people shall not oppress them any more."

This "place" is the land promised to Abraham (Genesis 12:7). And David has extended its boundaries beyond even those taken during Joshua's conquest. In his commentary on 2 Samuel, Peter Leithart suggests David doubled the size of the kingdom:

> "**Yahweh** gave Israel a place, and not just any place. He gave them a roomy place, a place to stretch out in."

David rules his world. He has defeated his enemies. He has given his people "rest" (7:11). And he establishes justice. **8:16-18** describes the officials who ensure a well-ordered kingdom. As a result: "David reigned over all Israel, doing what was just and right for all his people" (**v 15**). And by doing what is just and right, God's people commend the ways of God to the nations (Genesis 18:18-19).

2 Samuel **8:18** says, "David's son were priests". But priests were to be from the tribe of **Levi** and no one else could function as a priest—

not even the royal family, as Saul learnt to his cost in 1 Samuel 13. The only exception in 1 and 2 Samuel is Samuel himself—because of his prophetic ministry. The comment in 2 Samuel **8:18** comes without any explanation. We must assume that the writer intended this state-ment to raise questions in the mind of the reader—but not to provide an answer. At the end of a chapter of triumph it sounds an ominous note—especially given the track record of the sons of leaders in 1 Samuel 2:12-17 and **8:1-5.** David's reign is not going to be the final fulfilment of the promise in Psalm 2.

Psalm 2 describes the victory of God's king. But it pushes us beyond David to the *ultimate* Christ: Jesus. Jesus is the great conqueror. He has conquered our greatest enemies: the **nexus** of sin, Satan and death. He took them on at the cross and extinguished their power.

"The sting of death is sin, and the power of sin is the law. But thanks be to God! He gives us the victory through our Lord Jesus Christ." (1 Corinthians 15:56-57)

"[God] forgave us all our sins, having cancelled the charge of our legal indebtedness, which stood against us and condemned us; he has taken it away, nailing it to the cross. And having disarmed the powers and authorities, he made a public spectacle of them, triumphing over them by the cross." (Colossians 2:13-15)

"Since the children have flesh and blood, [Jesus] too shared in their humanity so that by his death he might break the power of him who holds the power of death—that is, the devil—and free those who all their lives were held in slavery by their fear of death." (Hebrews 2:14-15)

Jesus has ascended into heaven to receive an eternal kingdom in fulfil-ment of 2 Samuel 7. And just as David ruled the four corners of his world, so Jesus rules the four corners of the world. The ends of the earth belong to Christ. At the moment he rules from heaven. But one day he will return and establish his rule on earth. This is why we pray, "Your kingdom come, your will be done on earth as it is in heaven" (Matthew 6:10).

To the rule of Christ, there are two responses. We are presented with two options: serve the King or scorn the King. They are described in Psalm 2 and illustrated in 2 Samuel 9 and 10.

The Sensible Response: Serve the King

Psalm 2:10-12 says:

> "Therefore, you kings, be wise;
> > be warned, you rulers of the earth.
> Serve the LORD with fear
> > and celebrate his rule with trembling.
> Kiss his son …
> > Blessed are all who take refuge in him."

This is how the psalmist applies the story of David and the coming of the ultimate Christ. "Therefore, you kings, be wise," says verse 10. This is wisdom: to serve the LORD with fear, to kiss his son. And those who submit find refuge in him. This is what we see in chapter 9.

Some years into his reign, David wants to ensure he is keeping his promise to Jonathan to look after his family (2 Samuel **9:1**; 1 Samuel 20:11-17). Ziba, an old servant of Saul's household, is asked whether any of Saul's family are still alive (2 Samuel **9:2-3**). He tells David about Mephibosheth, the disabled son of Jonathan (4:4), and so Mephibosheth is summoned (**9:4-5**). Jonathan had said to David, "Do not ever cut off your kindness from my family—not even when the LORD has cut off every one of David's enemies from the face of the earth" (1 Samuel 20:15). Now David's enemies are being cut off. Perhaps Mephibosheth fears the same fate (2 Samuel **9:6**). He bows before David in complete humility (**v 8**). But David has sworn not to "cut off" Jonathan's descendants (1 Samuel 24:21-22). Mephibosheth's land may have been confiscated after Saul's fall or Ziba may have taken the opportunity to appropriate it (the text highlights Ziba's wealth in

> Don't be afraid.
> Eat at my table.
> Be like a son.

2 Samuel **9:10** and his later actions in 16:1-4 and 19:24-30 are at best ambiguous). Now David restores Mephibosheth's land (**9:7**), commissioning Ziba to manage it (**v 9-11**), and gives Mephibosheth a place in his household (**v 7, 13**). Jonathan's family lives on (**v 12**).

Mephibosheth is from the defeated family of Saul. He might well have had a chip on his shoulder, a grudge in his heart and maybe even a plan up his sleeve. But no, when he came before David, "he bowed down to pay him honour" and what he says is, "At your service" (**v 6**). And this, says Psalm 2, is wisdom. For Mephibosheth finds refuge with David. David's response is a picture of Christ's response to those who bow before him. David's response is:

1. Don't be afraid.

2. Eat at my table.

3. Be like a son.

Don't Be Afraid

Imagine what it was like for Mephibosheth to hear those words. He is summoned before the king. He has plenty of reasons to think David will have him killed. He can't fight and he can't run. And then David says, "Do not be afraid."

In verses 2 Samuel **9:1-5** and **verses 9-13** the writer refers to David as "the king". But in **verses 6-8**, in the conversation with Mephibosheth, he uses his personal name—David. It's not too fanciful to imagine that this reflects a change of tone in David's voice. He speaks to Mephibosheth not as the king, but as a friend of Mephibosheth's father and therefore a friend of the son. "I will surely show you kindness for the sake of your father Jonathan" (**v 7**). "Don't be afraid."

These words are echoed by the angel in Luke 2:9-11. The shepherds are terrified. But the angel says, "Do not be afraid" for he has come with "good news". And the good news is that a Saviour is born "in the town of David". "He is the Messiah." ('Messiah' is the

Hebrew word for "Christ".) God's anointed King is coming and it is good news for those who submit to him. "Don't be afraid."

These words are also echoed by Jesus himself in Matthew 28:10. The risen Jesus appears to the women who have come to his tomb and fall at his feet. But he says, "Do not be afraid".

Today the King of all the world says to you through his word, "Don't be afraid'.

Eat at My Table

Mephibosheth says: "At your service" (2 Samuel **9:6**). David responds:"...at my table". Indeed it is repeated four times in **verses 7, 10, 11** and **12**. David is not merely fulfilling the letter of his promise to Jonathan. Mephibosheth is not merely tolerated. He's not just given provisions. He's invited into a relationship with David. Eating is a powerful symbol of friendship. That was true then and it's still true today. That's why Jesus eating with "tax collectors and sinners" was so controversial. God's king was eating with God's enemies as a sign of God's grace.

It is the same today. Christ does not merely tolerate us. He invites us into a relationship of intimacy and friendship. And that is powerfully symbolised in the invitation to eat at his table in the Lord's Supper. Christ says to you, *Eat at my table*.

The bread and wine that we receive are a promise of Christ's grace to us. When we are weighed down by our sin, when we feel its guilt stabbing at our hearts, when we fear his wrath—he places in our hands bread and wine as a pledge of his love. We come with all our selfishness and self-pity, and Jesus says, *Eat at my table.*

Questions for reflection

1. Do you struggle with the thought of God's judgment on people, and how that is played out through warfare in the Old Testament? What thoughts from this chapter will help you with that?

2. "Don't be afraid." What are "good fears" and "bad fears" when we think about coming into the presence of the living, loving God?

3. "Eat at my table". Jesus has invited you to eat at his table: a sign of welcome and privilege. How will you use your table—meal times, eating together, food fellowship—to reflect and extend to others Jesus' invitation to belong to his family?

PART TWO

David is the all-conquering king who subdues the nations as God's christ. But Mephibosheth has no need to fear. He finds refuge at David's table. But David goes further.

Be Like a Son

"Mephibosheth ate at David's table like one of the king's sons" (**9:11**). Mephibosheth is treated like a royal son.

The meaning of "Mephibosheth" is unclear (it could mean "one who scatters shame" or "from the mouth of shame"). But what is clear is that it incorporates the word "shame" (just as Ish-Bosheth's name did). Moreover, Mephibosheth is currently living in Lo Debar (**v 7**) which means "No-Word" or "Nothing". He lives nowhere, a place so insignificant its name is No-Name. He is man of shame in a place of shame.

Mephibosheth offers his service to David, but he has no service he can really offer. Twice we're told "he was lame in both feet" (**v 3, 13**). Today he might have been given a wheelchair and a desk job. But this was an **agrarian** and military economy. Mephibosheth offers his service, but he cannot till his own land (**v 9-10**), let alone serve in David's fields or army. He describes himself as "a dead dog" (**v 8**). Mephibosheth is a nobody from nowhere with nothing to offer. And David treats him like a son.

Jesus told a story in which "the poor, the crippled, the blind and the lame" are invited to eat at the table of a great banquet (Luke 14:15-24). In the following chapter Jesus tells the story of a returning **prodigal** who, like Mephibosheth, offers to be a servant, but is treated as a son (15:17-24). The connection is easy to make. We are spiritually crippled with no service we can offer Jesus. But Jesus makes us sons and daughters of God. We are "in Christ", *in* God the Son. And that means we are loved by God the Father with the same love that he has for his own Son.

The word "kindness" in 2 Samuel **9:1, 3, 7** is *khesed,* which means "covenant faithfulness" or "loving kindness". We sometimes talk about the letter of the law. *Khesed* is the spirit of the law, the kindness that delights to fulfil covenant obligations. Back in 1 Samuel 20:14 Jonathan had said to David, "Show me unfailing kindness [*khesed*] like the LORD's kindness". David is keen to fulfil his covenant with Jonathan (2 Samuel **9:1, 7**). But he's also reflecting God's covenant faithfulness to him. In **verse 3** he asks, "Is there no one still alive from the house of Saul to whom I can show God's kindness?" David wants to extend the kindness that he has received (7:15).

> Our instinct should be to work out how we can extend to others the grace and loving kindness we have received in the gospel.

And now God's kindness has come to us. Titus 3:4 says, "the kindness and love of God our Saviour appeared" in the person of Jesus Christ. Our instinct should be the same—to work out how we can extend to others the grace and loving kindness we have received in the gospel.

The Foolish Response: Scorn the King

The first response to God's King suggested by Psalm 2 is to serve him and find refuge in him. This is the wise option. The second option is to scorn the King. The psalm begins with the kings of the earth saying, "Let us break their chains and throw off their shackles" (Psalm 2:3) This option leads to destruction. Psalm 2:10 and 12 say:

"Therefore, you kings, be wise ...
    Kiss his son, or he will be angry
        and your way will lead to your destruction,
        for his wrath can flare up in a moment."

This is what we see in 2 Samuel 10. Chapter 10 starts in the same way as chapter 9. At the beginning of chapter 9, David plans to show "kindness" to the house of Saul (**9:1**). At the beginning of chapter 10, David plans to show "kindness" to the house of Nahash, the **Ammonite** king (**10:1-2**). And if Hanun, Nahash's son, had been wise, then chapter 10 would have unfolded much as chapter 9 did, with David extending a gracious refuge. "Hanun" means "grace" or "favour" (like the name "Hannah"). But in this case it's ironic for Hanun is anything but gracious.

Hanun's father, Nahash, was defeated by Saul in 1 Samuel 11:1-11, but appears to have aided David at some (otherwise unrecorded) point during David's time as a fugitive (2 Samuel **10:2**). So David sends a delegation to express his sympathy when Nahash dies. But the Ammonites are suspicious of David's intentions (**v 3**). In effect they say, *Let us break their chains and throw off their shackles.*

And so they disgrace David's delegation by shaving off their beards (a sign of emasculation) and cutting off half their clothes to expose their buttocks (**v 4**). David does his best to minimise the humiliation to his men (**v 5**). Were its consequences not so serious, it would be akin to a schoolboy prank. But such humiliation of an ambassador is very serious indeed. This is not wisdom; it is foolishness.

The Ammonites realise their mistake and prepare for war by hiring Aramean mercenaries (**v 6**). The Arameans probably had their own agenda—control over the main north-south trade route. In response David sends out the entire army (**v 7**). The Ammonites and Arameans divide to envelope Israel in a **pincer movement** (**v 8**). So Joab, David's commander, divides his forces between himself and his brother, Abishai (**v 9-11**). He says:

> "Be strong, and let us fight bravely for our people and the cities of our God. The LORD will do what is good in his sight." (**v 12**)

This is the only time God is mentioned in the chapter. Whatever else his faults may have been (this is the first reference to him since his murder of Abner), Joab has faith in God. It is similar to **Shadrach, Meshach and Abednego's** statement that they will serve God whether he delivers from the furnace or not (Daniel 3:17-18). In any given situation, God may deliver us or he may not. He may intervene as we hope and he may not. But we can be confident that he will do what is good. And we can be confident in our ultimate, eternal salvation. And so we can be brave. We cannot fail—not ultimately.

When the Arameans flee before Joab (2 Samuel **10:13**), the Ammonites give up (**v 14**). The Aramean mercenaries regroup and call up reinforcements (**v 15-16**). Battle is re-engaged and David is victorious (**v 17-19**).

The chapter ends, "So the Arameans were afraid to help the Ammonites any more" (**v 19**). The word "afraid" is related to the word "to see" and the theme of "seeing" has run through the chapter. The Ammonites "saw" ("realised") that David had become their enemy (**v 6**). Joab "saw" the battle lines (**v 9**). The Ammonites "saw" ("realised") the Arameans had fled (**v 14**). The Ammonites regrouped when they "saw" that they had been defeated (**v 15**). The kings sued for peace when they "saw" they had been routed (**v 19**). To see who David is (or to see the God who fights for him) is to fear David (and the God who fights for him).

The Ammonites scorn God's king and they are defeated. The Arameans join the rebellion and they are defeated—twice. The story echoes the statements of Psalm 2: "The nations conspire … against the LORD and against his anointed." But they "plot in vain". This response to God's King "will lead to your destruction.'

God has given Jesus authority over the nations. And so Jesus sends us—his people—to the nations, commanding them to obey his rule (Matthew 28:18-20). This is what the mission of the church is. Jesus rules the four corners of the world and so he sends us to the four corners of the world. We extend the reign of Christ by proclaiming his kingdom.

Christ's rule is good news. But make no mistake: to reject his rule is bad news—very bad news indeed. God will establish his King. Today, the rulers of the earth are every one of us. More than ever, we run our own lives the way we choose. The most popular song played at funerals today is "I did it my way". But if you choose to ignore Christ, then "your way will lead to destruction" (Psalm 2:12).

In Romans 2:4-5 Paul says that God *delays* judgment because of his kindness. He is giving us time to repent. But we must not show contempt for his kindness, as Hanun did.

"Or do you show contempt for the riches of his kindness, tolerance and patience, not realising that God's kindness leads you towards repentance? But because of your stubbornness and your unrepentant heart, you are storing up wrath against yourself for the day of God's wrath, when his righteous judgment will be revealed." (Romans 2:4-5)

What hope is there for rebels against God's King? Psalm 2 ends like this: "Blessed are all who take refuge in him". We're all rebels against God. We've all tried to live our lives without him. We all deserve his judgment. But Christ himself provides a refuge from his own judgment. He took the judgment of his people on himself at the cross.

> One way or another, every knee will bow before Jesus.

Those who are willing to bow before the Son, God's anointed, and say, "At your service", will find a refuge in his family. But those who continue to rebel against the Son will be conquered when he returns at the end of history. They will be "subdued" just as David subdued the Philistines (2 Samuel **8:1**). Because, one way or another, every knee will bow before Jesus (Philippians 2:10).

Scorned for the King's Sake

You may no longer scorn the King. You may instead now be scorned for the King's sake. You may be like the delegation that David sent to Hanun. You may not have had your backside exposed, but in other, perhaps more subtle ways, you have been "greatly humiliated" (2 Samuel **10:5**). Your friends may have heaped abuse on you because you no longer join them in their reckless lifestyle (1 Peter 4:4). You may have to endure a daily round of mockery from colleagues, or wither inside each time you hear Christ's name scorned in your workplace. Your family may have opposed your faith. King David was concerned about the humiliation his servants endured (2 Samuel **10:5**). In the same way, Jesus is concerned about your suffering.

But we must also remember that we are humiliated for the sake of the Christ. What is happening to us is part of the larger pattern of humanity's hostility towards God's King, which came to a climax at the cross. The early church recognised that the rebellion against God's christ described in Psalm 2 came to its hideous fulfilment at the cross of the Christ, and continues in the persecution of the Christ's people. For it was Psalm 2 which they turned into prayer when they were first persecuted (Acts 4:25-29). Hanun did not take a personal dislike to the delegation. He disgraced *them* because of his antagonism towards *David*. And we, if we suffer as Christians, are suffering for *Christ's* sake.

And there is joy to be found in this realisation. In Acts 4 the church uses Psalm 2 to pray for boldness. Their prayer is answered with a Spirit-empowered boldness as they continue to preach Christ. As a result the apostles are brought before the **Sanhedrin** and told to stop—something they refuse to do. Acts 5:41 says, "The apostles left the Sanhedrin, rejoicing because they had been counted worthy of suffering disgrace for the Name". Suffering becomes a curious confirmation that we are united with Christ (1 Peter 4:12-13).

One final point to note: David is "the christ", God's anointed king. He prefigures "the Christ", God's ultimate King, Jesus. But David himself is *not* God's ultimate King. In chapter 11 we are about to see him falling into sin. He will not be the king that he should be. And there is perhaps a hint of what is to come in chapter 10. There is a lot of dividing into two in this chapter. Beards are shaved in half (**v 4**). Garments are cut in the middle (**v 4**). Armies are split into two (**v 8, 9-10**). Even the battle itself takes place in two rounds (**v 13-16**). Perhaps it is meant to foreshadow what will happen in David's family in chapters 11 – 20 because of David's sin.

Questions for reflection

1. You have received the loving kindness of God in his Son: Jesus. How can you share that with others today?

2. Do you have friends, family, work colleagues, neighbours who openly "scorn the king"? How can you pray for them? How is silent indifference also a form of scorning King Jesus? How can you pray for them?

3. What kind of persecution do you receive for Jesus' sake? If you are being persecuted, how can you remain joyful? If you are not being persecuted, why do you think that might be?

6. FOUR STEPS TO DEATH: FOUR STEPS TO FREEDOM

Could you deliberately kill someone?

Could you reach a point in your life when in cold blood you plotted someone's murder? You don't think so? 2 Samuel 11 starts with David—a successful king, a lover of God, a man who has been searching for peace in his land, who has seen so much blessing as he has trusted the Lord—wandering on a rooftop enjoying the fresh air. Just 13 verses later he is arranging a wicked murder. This is David, God's anointed king, the man after God's heart. And he murders an innocent man. It's as if we stop viewing David the messiah-king, and see David the man underneath—and it's not pretty.

How does this happen? We should want to know for fear it might happen to us.

Four Steps to Death

David didn't decide to murder Uriah in a single moment. He was drawn into sin step by step. Even if your path doesn't end in murder, it may end with the destruction of your soul. For, one way or another, sin leads to death. James says, "After desire has conceived, it gives birth to sin; and sin, when it is full-grown, gives birth to death" (James 1:15). This is a life-and-death issue.

Step One: Neglecting Our Duty

The scary thing is that the whole process starts with nothing. David didn't make an intentional step towards evil. The story begins in 2 Samuel **11:1** with David neglecting his duty as king to lead the army. Step one involves doing nothing.

How does this lead to further sin? Not serving as we should makes us unhappy, and discontentment makes us vulnerable to temptation. I realise this is counter-intuitive, but let's think it through. We think that pleasing ourselves will make us happy. But Jesus says the opposite:

"Then he called the crowd to him along with his disciples and said: 'Whoever wants to be my disciple must deny themselves and take up their cross and follow me. For whoever wants to save their life will lose it, but whoever loses their life for me and for the gospel will save it.'" (Mark 8:34-35)

Self-denial and service bring true satisfaction because this is what we were made for. Think of the people in your church who are happiest, and think of those who serve most. More often than not, you'll find they're the same people.

When you curtail your service, you become unhappy. When you become unhappy, you become vulnerable to temptation. You're left wide open to the false promises of sin. But, when you have joy in Christ, the enticements of sin fall on deaf ears.

Step Two: Indulging Our Eyes

The story continues:

"One evening David got up from his bed and walked around on the roof of the palace. From the roof he saw a woman bathing. The woman was very beautiful, and David sent someone to find out about her. The man said, 'She is Bathsheba, the daughter of Eliam and the wife of Uriah the **Hittite**?'" (2 Samuel **11:2-3**)

I don't know whether David went on the roof to spy on naked women. I suspect not. I don't know whether Bathsheba was hoping to be seen. I suspect not. But David did see Bathsheba naked, and instead of looking away, he indulged himself. He didn't flee temptation. He saw, and he longed for what he saw.

It was the Garden of Eden all over again:

"When the woman saw that the fruit of the tree was good for food and pleasing to the eye, and also desirable for gaining wisdom, she took some and ate it. She also gave some to her husband, who was with her, and he ate it." (Genesis 3:6)

What Adam and Eve thought was good was determined not by God's word, but by what they saw. They lived by sight and not by faith.

God has just made a covenant with David which is a covenant for the human race (2 Samuel 7:19). From David's descendants will come the new Adam, who will restore humanity. But David is not that new Adam. He proves to be like the old Adam. He's led by sight rather than by faith.

> Self-denial and service bring true satisfaction because this is what we were made for.

David's sin was not to *see* Bathsheba; his sin was to *keeping on looking*. Where do your eyes wander? Perhaps you look at porn on the internet. Perhaps you watch rom-coms when you know they'll make you discontented. Perhaps you look at someone who's not your spouse and indulge your fantasies. Or maybe for you it's not sexual temptation. Maybe you see adverts for cars or clothes, for houses or holidays, and let those adverts shape your longings, hopes and dreams. You're led by sight rather than by faith. You think you'll be happy only if you go on the holiday, buy the car or have the latest accessories. The gospel offers you joy in Christ. But you follow your eyes and, in the end, are dissatisfied with God's goodness. You convince yourself that God is not enough.

Step Three: Betraying Our Spouses

The result is adultery.

"Then David sent messengers to get her. She came to him, and he slept with her." (**11:4**)

■ *Spiritual Adultery.* The Bible talks about our relationship with Christ as a marriage. We're united to him just as a man and woman are united in marriage. So to replace love for Christ with something or someone else is spiritual adultery. The sign of this is that we disobey Christ. We put something else first because that thing matters more to us than Christ. "At least that's not as bad literal adultery," you may say. But actually *it's worse*. To betray your spouse is terrible, but to betray God is worse. And spiritual adultery is the root of all other sins. You're opening a **Pandora's box** of sin.

■ *Heart Adultery.* Heart adultery is one specific form of spiritual adultery. Jesus said: "You have heard that it was said, 'You shall not commit adultery.' But I tell you that anyone who looks at a woman lustfully has already committed adultery with her in his heart" (Matthew 5:27-28). You can commit adultery without having intercourse: an indulged infatuation; a fantasy affair; a lustful undressing with the eyes; a porn habit.

■ *Physical Adultery.* Perhaps it's gone beyond heart adultery to physical adultery. The mundane realities of having small children have made your marriage seem dull—certainly when compared with the excitement of an affair. Or perhaps your spouse is not all you hoped they might be and so you've looked elsewhere. Perhaps singleness became more than you felt you could endure, especially when you saw friends getting married. So now you've persuaded yourself that you have a right to what everyone else has. Or perhaps you have no idea how you ended up where you are, but here you are in adultery.

Step Four: Hiding Our Sin

David's next move is a classic act of politics and power—a cover-up.

"The woman conceived and sent word to David, saying, 'I am pregnant.' So David sent this word to Joab: 'Send me Uriah the Hittite.' And Joab sent him to David." (2 Samuel **11:5-6**)

David recalls Uriah from the battlefield, hoping Uriah will sleep with Bathsheba so they can pass off the baby as Uriah's. The problem is, Uriah refuses to go home while his comrades are at war (**v 7-9**). When David asks why he will not go home (**v 10**), Uriah replies:

"The ark and Israel and Judah are staying in tents, and my commander Joab and my lord's men are camped in the open country. How could I go to my house to eat and drink and make love to my wife? As surely as you live, I will not do such a thing!" (**v 11**)

It's hard not to hear this as a rebuke to the king who had stayed at home. David's next step is to get Uriah drunk, but still Uriah will not go home (**v 12-13**).

Perhaps this is where you are: hiding sin from others. Think about the following questions seriously and honestly:

- What's your secret sin?

- How do you hide it from others?

- How long have you been hiding?

- What are the results of this hiding? What toll is it taking on you, your relationships and your relationship with God?

Death

The next step for David is murder. He sends Uriah back to the battlefront with a sealed message that is Uriah's own death warrant (**v 14-15**). David tells Joab to attack the city wall and then retreat leaving Uriah exposed in battle (**v 16-25**). David sets up a situation that will inevitably lead to Uriah's death. Then, with Uriah out of the way, he can marry Bathsheba and hope no one does the sums too closely (**v 26-27**). It all has a cold logic to it from David's point of view—if you are able to forget about the LORD.

> Conscience is the internal alarm system that God has fitted within us to stop us sinning.

We are all four steps from murder. Perhaps you find the thought that you might murder someone inconceivable. But conceive of it! You may not be one step from murder, but you are four steps from murder.

Or consider this. How many murders would be committed if there were no punishment, no consequences? Would you commit murder if it remained a secret, if there were no ramifications for you? Maybe the only difference between you and David is that you fear the consequences of murder more than he did? The Lord Jesus raises the stakes for us considerably in the Sermon on the Mount. Maybe the same murderous intent is in your heart:

> "You have heard that it was said to the people long ago, 'You shall not murder, and anyone who murders will be subject to judgment.' But I tell you that anyone who is angry with a brother or sister will be subject to judgment. Again, anyone who says to a brother or sister, '**Raca**,' is answerable to the court. And anyone who says, 'You fool!' will be in danger of the fire of hell."

> (Matthew 5:21-22)

1 Timothy 4:2 talks about people "whose consciences have been seared as with a hot iron". My grandfather was a steel worker. He routinely came home with burns up his arms. After repeated burns his skin became hard and lost sensitivity. Paul says the same thing can happen to your conscience. Conscience is the internal alarm system that God has fitted within us to stop us sinning. Whenever we're tempted to sin, our conscience screams at us to stop. It makes us uneasy and hesitant. Think where you would be without conscience. But Paul says that if you push past your conscience enough times then the

alarm stops ringing—or we stop listening. Our conscience becomes seared, hardened, insensitive. And that's a truly terrible situation to be in.

It might not be murder. But sin can take you down paths you would never have dreamed of walking. Nobody decides one day to have an affair. Nobody decides one day to steal from their company. But if you neglect your duty, if you gratify your eyes, if you indulge your fantasies, if you fail to flee temptation—then that may be where you end up.

"I would never do that," you may be thinking. But please don't think you're better than David. Remember, this is God's anointed king, the man after God's own heart, the writer of great psalms of faith, the one to whom God spoke directly. He was a better man than you—and he fell, catastrophically. David didn't think of himself as a potential murderer. He didn't wake up at the beginning of 2 Samuel 11 with murder on his mind. It was a thousand miles from his thoughts. Yet murder is where he ended up. He didn't get there in one step. But it only took four steps.

Questions for reflection

1. Where are you now in the four steps? Neglecting your duty? Indulging your eyes? Betraying your spouse? Hiding your sin? What will you do about it?

2. "Self-denial and service bring true satisfaction because this is what we were made for." Do you believe this? How will you respond to this challenge?

3. How can we help others who are caught up somewhere in the four steps? How can you help a friend talk honestly about a sin they are caught up in and feel trapped by? How will you encourage and advise them?

PART TWO

Four Steps to Freedom

Step One: Exposed by God's Word

David thinks he's got away with it. But he's exposed by God's word. For David, this came through the prophet Nathan. Nathan comes to David and tells a story of a poor man who had a little lamb which was like a daughter to him. But then a rich neighbour seizes the lamb to serve to his guests (**12:1-4**). "David," we're told," burned with anger" when he heard this story (**v 5-6**).

Then Nathan comes out with his devastating punchline: "You are the man!" (**v 7**). It's one of the great moments in the Bible. Nathan exposes David in a wonderful sideways move. Often a full-on assault leads only to defensiveness. Self-justification is our instinctive response. But David is undone and condemned by his own words. "To cut away diseased tissue in David's heart and heal the wound there," says **Augustine**, "Nathan used David's tongue as a knife" (*Explanations of the Psalms 50*). Nathan's story is in fact a **parable** of David's life. "I gave you all Israel and Judah," says God. "And if all this had been too little, I would have given you even more" (**v 8**). It's an echo of David's prayer in 7:18-19. But David has despised God's generosity (**12:9**). He has become the godless king of whom Samuel had warned—the kind of king who takes from the people (1 Samuel 8:10-18), rather than serving them.

Joab's speech to the messenger who would bring the news of Uriah has already implied as much (2 Samuel **11:18-21**). Joab puts words in David's mouth, imagining him complaining that the army has been negligent in allowing someone to be killed so close to the wall. Joab imagines David likening this to **Abimelek**, who was killed when a woman dropped a stone on his head in Judges 9. To the messenger it was probably simply an example of a foolish battle strategy. But to the readers of Samuel it's clear that it's David (not Uriah) who is like

Abimelek: a king who takes what's not his and kills his brothers to do so. It's David (not Uriah) who deserves Abimelek's fate.

In 2 Samuel 7 God had promised to establish David's "house"—in the sense of dynasty. But now in judgment, the sword will never leave David's "house"—in the sense of family (**12:10-12**).

For David, God's word came through a prophet. For you, it might come through reading the Scriptures, through a talk or sermon at church, or through the rebuke of a friend. Hebrews 4:12-13 says:

"The word of God is alive and active. Sharper than any double-edged sword, it penetrates even to dividing soul and spirit, joints and marrow; it judges the thoughts and attitudes of the heart. Nothing in all creation is hidden from God's sight. Everything is uncovered and laid bare before the eyes of him to whom we must give account."

You can hide your sin from people, but you cannot hide your sin from God. And God comes to you through his word, seeking you out, exposing your sin, inviting you to leave the road that leads to death and step towards freedom. Reading 2 Samuel 11 – 12 may be God's call to you to repent. If you have a secret sin, God is saying, *You are the man ... You are the woman.* This is your opportunity to step towards freedom.

Step Two: Helped by God's People

We mustn't minimise Nathan's role in this. First, Nathan challenges David (**12:7**). Second, Nathan hears David's confession. Third, Nathan reassures David. **Verse 13** says: "Then David said to Nathan, 'I have sinned against the LORD.'" Nathan replied, 'The LORD has taken away your sin. You are not going to die.'"

Notice how David confesses "to Nathan". David doesn't say, "I'll think about what you've said and perhaps pray about it". David doesn't quietly confess his sin to God and hope no one else finds out. David confesses his sin to Nathan. If you tell yourself, "I don't need to tell other people because I can sort this out on my own", then what you're really saying is, "I don't really want to give up this sin". I have been a pastor too long—and I myself have been a sinner too long—to be fooled by that claim. It's hiding, and we hide so we can continue to sin.

Or if you hide your sin, you're putting your reputation before your holiness. Being *thought of* as a holy person matters more to you than *being* a holy person. God gave us the Christian community to help us change. And you need that help. You need accountability. Telling a mature Christian friend is a crucial step towards true repentance, forgiveness, assurance and freedom.

Step Three: Welcomed by God's Grace

God's word issues a call to you to come to him in repentance. But to come, you need to be confident that God will welcome you and forgive you. This is so important. The gospel is not a word of condemnation. It's a word of invitation. Yes, it exposes us and warns us. Yes, it will ultimately judge those who resist its call. But for now, it's a gracious word of invitation. If your main impression of this story is that it is very challenging, then you've missed the point. First and foremost, it's an invitation to turn from sin to God's grace.

In some ways, David's sin is greater than Saul's. Saul disobeyed the spoken word of a prophet. David disobeyed the written word of the law of the LORD. Saul did not commit adultery and, while he plotted murder against David, he was unable to carry it through. Yet it was Saul who lost his kingdom. What makes the difference is David's repentance. And what enabled David's repentance was his faith in God's grace.

David reaction is in marked contrast to Saul's. When the prophet Samuel confronted Saul, Saul was evasive and made excuses (1 Samuel 15:13-21). David says, "I have sinned against the LORD". This is the key step. There's no true forgiveness without genuine repentance. No excuses. No minimising your sin. "'I have sinned'," wrote Augustine, "is just three syllables; and yet in these three **syllables** the flames of the heart's sacrifice rose up to heaven" (Sermon 393.1). As a result of those three syllables, Nathan says to David, "The LORD has taken away your sin. You are not going to die" (2 Samuel **12:13**).

> Telling a mature Christian friend is a crucial step towards true repentance, forgiveness, assurance and freedom.

In AD 390 the people of Thessalonica rioted in protest at having pagan Goths garrisoned near their city, and the garrison commander was murdered. In retaliation the Roman emperor, Theodosius I, ordered the garrison to kill all the spectators in the city's **circus**. As a result, Ambrose, the godly bishop of Milan, **excommunicated** the emperor and wrote a bold letter calling on him to repent:

"Are you ashamed, sir, to do as David did—David, the king and the prophet, the ancestor of Christ according to the flesh? ... Therefore do not take it ill, sir, if what was said to King David is said to you, "You are the man." For if you listen with attention and say, "I have sinned against the Lord" ... then it will be said to you also, "Because you repented, the Lord has put away your sin: you shall not die." (Letter 51.7)

A few months later Ambrose duly readmitted Theodosius to the church, after he had publicly repented.

We have David's prayer of confession in Psalm 51. The superscription reads, "A psalm of David. When the prophet Nathan came to him after David had committed adultery with Bathsheba."

"Have mercy on me, O God,
    according to your unfailing love;
    according to your great compassion
    blot out my transgressions ...
"Cleanse me with **hyssop**, and I shall be clean;

> wash me, and I shall be whiter than snow ...
>> My sacrifice, O God, is a broken spirit;
>> a broken and contrite heart,
>> you, God, will not despise." (Psalm 51:1, 7, 17)

It's because David trusts in God's "unfailing love" and his "great compassion" that David comes before God. He comes trusting that God *can* cleanse him and *will* cleanse him. And if God cleanses him then he'll "be whiter than snow". God will not despise "a broken and contrite heart".

If you think of God simply as the Judge or the King then you'll never come to him. You'll hide your sin from him. But God is the Father, who loves you with "unfailing love" and "great compassion". His mercy is greater than your sin—even if you've committed adultery and murder. If you come to him with a broken heart, he will not despise you. He will be gentle with you and "restore to [you] the joy of your salvation" (v 12).

As we've noted, Hebrews says the word of God exposes us. "Everything is uncovered and laid bare before the eyes of him to whom we must give account" (4:12). But the writer goes on:

> "Therefore, since we have a great high priest who has ascended into heaven, Jesus the Son of God, let us hold firmly to the faith we profess. For we do not have a high priest who is unable to sympathise with our weaknesses, but we have one who has been tempted in every way, just as we are—yet he did not sin. Let us then approach the throne of grace with confidence, so that we may receive mercy and find grace to help us in our time of need." (Hebrews 4:14-16)

The One who sees us is the One who offers grace in time of need.

We don't need to fear being exposed because the One who sees us is the One who sympathises with our weaknesses and offers grace in time of need.

Nevertheless, there is a death. Sin

always leads to death. David himself says, "As surely as the LORD lives, the man who did this must die" (2 Samuel **12:5**). And this is true. "The wages of sin is death," says Paul (Romans 6:23). Someone must die.

Imagine you are Uriah's father or Bathsheba's mother. How do you react when Nathan says to David, "The LORD has taken away your sin. You are not going to die"? Imagine today if a judge said to a rapist and murderer, "You're forgiven"? Crimes that are ignored or belittled evoke our moral outrage. "Where's the justice?" we cry. Where's the justice in this story?

You might think that "four steps to death" would be matched by "four steps to life". But I've called stage two "four steps to freedom" because this story does end with death. David's child pays the price. Nathan says in 2 Samuel **12:14**: "But because by doing this you have show utter contempt for LORD, the son born to you will die". Uriah's father loses a son. In return David loses a son. You might, of course, wonder whether that's fair on David's son. But notice how David is confident that his son will live on in eternity. When the child becomes ill (**v 15**), David fasts and pleads with God for the child (**v 16-17**). But when the child dies (**v 18**), David ends his mourning (**v 19-20**). When his attendants ask him about this change of attitude (**v 21**), David expresses his confidence that he will see the child again (**v 22-23**). Nevertheless the story ends with death.

It's a pointer to the cross. David sinned and deserved to die, but someone else died in his place. Not only that, but it was David's son who died (**v 14**). And one day the ultimate Son born to David's line, Jesus, would die for the sins of the world.

When David was finally appointed king in 5:1-3, the tribes of Israel said, "We are your own flesh and blood". It's literally "We're your own bone and flesh". As we've seen, it echoes Genesis 2, where Adam says Eve is "bone of my bone and flesh of my flesh". In other words, David is a husband to Israel. But David is an adulterous husband. He's betrayed, deceived and murdered Israel. We're left waiting for the true husband of God's people—Jesus. And Jesus lays down his life for his bride (Ephesians 5:25).

God forgives us, but somebody dies and that person was Jesus, David's greater son. He died for us, and his death is God's great declaration of welcome. It's at the cross that we see that God is a God of "unfailing love" and "great compassion", who does "not despise" those who come to him with "a broken heart" (Psalm 51:1, 17).

Bathsheba goes on to give birth to a second son, the son who will become David's immediate successor (2 Samuel **12:24**). David names him "Solomon". But God names him "Jedidiah", which means "loved by the LORD" because "the LORD loved him" (**v 24-25**).

We're welcomed by God's grace to God's love. Look at the cross and see the arms of God spread wide to embrace you. Confess your sin. Hear his reassurance in the gospel. Taste his grace in bread and wine. Come to God to find forgiveness and freedom.

Step Four: Restored to God's Service

The story began with David neglecting his duty as king. It ends with Joab calling him to the battlefront (**v 26-28**). David goes to lead his people to victory (**v 29-31**). David is restored to God's service. He acts like a king again.

Christians are called and destined to reign with the Christ, proclaiming his kingdom to a needy world. But you may be hamstrung in that service by secret sin. You don't need to be. You can be set free to be the person God has made you to be. You can be fit for purpose. All you need to do is confess your sin. And, looking to the cross, you can confess your sin with every confidence that God will receive you with "unfailing love" and "great compassion". Confession does not bring an end to Christian service. It brings about the beginning of restoration to service. This is why David's prayer of confession in Psalm 51 broadens out at the end from David's personal story to the story

of God's people. Through repentance David is restored to his service
as king.

> "Then I will teach transgressors your ways, so that
>> sinners will turn back to you …
> Open my lips, Lord
>> and my mouth will declare your praise …
> May it please you to prosper Zion
>> to build up the walls of Jerusalem." (Psalm 51:13, 15, 18)

At first I called this chapter "four steps to death". Then I thought
that maybe I should call it "four steps to freedom". But the reality
is that what this chapter is about is up to you. Has it described your
movement towards death? Or will it describe your movement towards
freedom?

Questions for reflection

1. *Exposed by God's word.* Are you putting yourself in a place, reg-
   ularly, where God will speak to you—even though you may be
   avoiding him because of some secret sin?

2. *Helped by God's people.* Do you have friendships, partnerships
   and relationships where you will be challenged and accountable
   for your life and actions? In what practical ways can you be avail-
   able to help others who may be struggling?

3. *Restored to God's service.* How should we help those who have
   failed, and encourage them back into service? What steps might
   they and the church need to make to help them?

7. THE FALL OF DAVID AND THE RISE OF ABSALOM

There are some stories they never teach in Sunday School and this sordid tale is one of them. It's the story of a godless act—a story made more poignant by the fact that God gets no mention.

A Godless Story

It begins with Amnon, one of David's sons, becoming "obsessed" with his half-sister Tamar (**13:2**), a relationship clearly forbidden in the Mosaic law (Leviticus 18:9). But the story of Amnon and Tamar is actually introduced: "Now Absalom, David's son, had a beautiful sister, whose name was Tamar" (2 Samuel **13:1**, ESV). In other words, this is really the beginning of the story of Absalom—even though he doesn't reappear until **verse 20**.

As we've seen, David offered to build a house (a temple) for God. But instead God promised to build a house (a dynasty) for David. But David's sin brings a sword to his house (family). David is forgiven, but his sin continues to have consequences. David can't restrain his sons because his moral authority has eroded. There's no direct or complete correlation between parents and their children, but bad parenting usually leads to wayward children. Passive fathers lead to rebellious sons (as was the case with Eli and Samuel in 1 Samuel 2:12-17 and 8:1-5). In 2 Samuel **13:1** both Absalom and Amnon are called "son of David". "Son of" obviously denotes parentage. But in Hebrew it can also denote a characteristic. "Son of wickedness" means "a wicked person". Absalom and Amnon are about to display the worst characteristics of David: Amnon sinning sexually like David with Bathsheba; Absalom committing murder like David against Uriah.

The story is made up of seven interlocking scenes, each with two characters, one of whom is part of the next scene: Jonadab-Amnon, Amnon-David, David-Tamar, Tamar-Amnon, Amnon-attendant, attendant-Tamar, Tamar-Absalom. The centre of the story is the encounter between Tamar and Amnon.

A Sorry Tale

Amnon's cousin, Jonadab, sees Amnon pining and offers advice (**v 3-4**). His motives are unclear. He reappears in **verses 32-33** as a confidante of Absalom. He's a meddler with no moral compass other than ingratiating himself. He's described as "very shrewd" (**v 3**). But he reminds us of the danger of choosing people with skills over people with godly character. Following Jonadab's advice, Amnon pretends to be ill (**v 5-6**), easily done since he's already said to be ill with his obsession (**v 2**). Amnon persuades David to send Tamar to attend to him (**v 6-7**). In 11:2 David was in bed and then had Bathsheba brought to his bedroom (v 4). Amnon now mimics this. Amnon is following his father's lead in all the wrong ways.

Tamar comes to bake for Amnon as he lies on his "sick" bed. The word translated "baked" in **13:8** can also mean to make the heart flutter. In Song of Songs 4:9 it is translated, "You have stolen my heart, my sister, my bride; you have stolen my heart". The words "send everyone out of here" in 2 Samuel **13:9** were used by Joseph in Genesis 45:1 as a preface to fraternal reconciliation. Here they will lead to **fratricide**.

In 2 Samuel **13:2** Amnon couldn't find a way "to do anything to her". This phrase has clear negative connotations. Alone with Tamar, Amnon can do what he wants "to" her (**v 10-11**). Tamar protests. The phrase "Don't do this wicked thing!" in **verse 12** echoes Genesis 34:7 (which also led to murderous vengeance) and Judges 19:23 (which leads to civil war). The incestuous marriage that Tamar suggests in 2 Samuel **13:13** would have been illegal, but perhaps Tamar thought she could buy time, or that an illegal marriage would be better than rape. But Amnon ignores her protests and rapes her (**v 14**).

With this terrible act of incestuous rape everything is turned upside down. Before, Amnon ordered his servants out so he could be alone with Tamar (**v 9**). Afterwards, he orders them back so they can remove her (**v 17**). Before, he told her, "Come lie down," while she begged to leave (**v 11-12**). Afterwards, he reverses this and says, "Get up and get out!" while she begs to stay (**v 15-16**) ("Sending away" in **verse 16** is an **idiom** for divorce.) Before, he "loved" her (**v 1**). Afterwards, he hates her (**v 15**). In **Verse 17** he literally says, "Get this out of here". Tamar has become a discarded object. The narrative is skilfully constructed:

a. Amnon "loves" Tamar (v 1-4)

   b. Tamar comes to Amnon and uses a fire to bake bread (**v 5-9**)

      c. Amnon orders his servants out so he can be with Tamar (**v 9-10**)

         d. Ignoring Tamar's pleas, Amnon says, "Come to bed with me" (**v 11-13**)

           e. Amnon hates Tamar after raping her (**v 14-15**)

         d*. Ignoring Tamar's pleas, Amnon says, "Get up and get out" (**v 15-16**)

      c*. Amnon orders his servants in so he can be without Tamar (**v 17-18**)

   b*. Tamar leaves Amnon and uses a fire's ashes to mourn (**v 19**)

a*. Absalom hates Amnon (**v 20-22**)

Tamar herself gives us the true perspective on this crime in **verses 12-13,** where the word "wicked" is literally "godless". "He was stronger than she," says **verse 14**. Throughout history men have used their strength to abuse women. Still today, domestic violence occurs across all sectors of society. And not for the last time, the victim here is cruelly blamed for an act of sexual violence (**v 15**). Tamar is right: such action is godless. She is left a desolate woman (**13:20**). It's the language used of a ruined city. Violence against women is godless.

Verse 21 says, "When King David heard all this, he was furious". The surprise about this verse is not what it says. David's fury is entirely justified. The surprise is that nothing then happens. It's anger without justice. David is too compromised. He himself has just been exposed as an adulterer and murderer—so what can he do?

> The surprise is that nothing then happens. It's anger without justice. David is too compromised.

The story starts with Amnon's "love" and ends with Absalom's anger (**v 22**). But this is calculating anger. "Don't take this thing to heart," Absalom tells Tamar (**v 20**). But this is precisely what he himself does. Absalom hides his anger (**v 22**), waiting for the chance to exact not justice, but revenge. Two years later Absalom makes his move. He invites the king to a party, apparently counting on David not attending (**v 23-25**). So Absalom makes David his go-between to lure Amnon just as Abner made David his go-between to lure Tamar (**v 26-27**). In an ugly parody of Joshua 1:9, Absalom orders his men to kill Amnon at his command (2 Samuel **13:28-29**). David is initially told that all his sons are dead (**v 30-31**). But Jonadab is on hand, apparently privy to Absalom's true intent (**v 32-36**). His words—"Let not my lord the king so take it to heart" (**v 33**, ESV)—echo Absalom's words to Tamar in **verse 20**.

Verses 37 and 39 are ambiguous. In **verse 37** David mourns for his son. But which son? Absalom goes into exile (**v 38**) and **verse 39** could mean, "King David longed to go against Absalom (in pursuit of justice) because he was grieved by Amnon's death." Or it could mean, "King David longed to go to Absalom, for he was consoled concerning (i.e. *by*) Amnon's death" (NIV). David's subsequent actions suggest the latter.

The return of Absalom

Joab makes the next move (**14:1-3**). His motives are unclear. Perhaps he fears Absalom will foment rebellion while he is absent. If so, this calculation will badly backfire. He enlists a "wise woman" of **Tekoa** and instructs her to "act like a woman who has spent many days grieving for the dead" (**v 2**). This mirrors David himself, who in **13:37** "mourned many days for his son". In the dialogue the woman pushes David until the trap is ready to be shut tight. She tells the story of a son who has killed his brother in an argument—what we might call man-slaughter today (**14:4-6**). Her clan is demanding vengeance, though she hints that their real motive is to steal her family's inheritance (**v 7**). David's initial response in **verse 8** is vague, the equivalent of "I'll look into it". Perhaps anticipating that David fears taking on the guilt of allowing the guilty to be unpunished, the woman says, "On me be the guilt" (**v 9** ESV). As a result David offers her protection (**v 10**). But it's still not specific to her "son" so the woman pleads that her son "not be destroyed" (**v 11**). Finally in **verse 12** David guarantees the life of the son, and the trap is sprung.

David has offered protection to a fratricidal son. But David has not protected his own fratricidal son (**v 13-14**). The woman shifts from her family story to the national story, but retains the language of inheritance. The implication is that David himself is going to "cut off" the woman, her son and the rest of Israel from their rightful inheritance— the rule of Absalom upon David's death (**v 15-17**). David rightly detects Joab's hand in this (**v 18-20**), and so addresses the command rehabilitating Absalom directly to Joab (**v 21-22**). Absalom can return, but may not see the king (**v 23-24**).

Twice the woman says David "has wisdom like that an angel" in "discerning good and evil" (**v 20, 17**). It's loaded with irony. For she is the "wise woman" (**v 3**) who has just tricked David into acting unwisely. Moreover in chapter 11 David did not discern good and evil, and in chapter 13 he failed to act when he did discern evil.

Just as Nathan had told a story in chapter 12 which invoked David's instinct for justice, now the woman of Tekoa has told a story that invokes his compassion. Both Nathan and the woman tell stories that mirror David's situation. But there is a crucial difference. David realised that God's hand was in Nathan's story. But here he correctly detects Joab's hand in the story (**14:19**). The result of Nathan's story is repentance and justice. The result of Joab's story will prove to be much more ambiguous.

A Crown of Beauty Instead of Ashes

Where is God in this "godless" story in which he doesn't get a mention? He is fulfilling his word of judgment. This story comes immediately after David's taking of Bathsheba. Nathan had said, "Now, therefore, the sword shall never depart from your house, because you despised me and took the wife of Uriah the Hittite to be your own" (12:10). Now the sword has entered David's house. In a godless world we can be sure that God will fulfil his word: both his word of judgment and of salvation.

David is the christ, God's anointed king, Israel's greatest king. But in the end he's a let-down. 2 Samuel leaves us longing for a king who will exercise justice without hypocrisy—a king with moral authority. We need a king who can say to the baying crowd as again they accuse the victim, "Let him who is without sin cast the first stone" (John 8:7). We need Jesus.

But King Jesus does more than execute justice. He also covers our shame. "Where could I get rid of my disgrace?" asks Tamar before her rape (2 Samuel **13:13**). The answer will be *at the cross*. At the cross, Jesus not only atoned for our guilt; he also removed our shame. He puts right both the wrong we have done and the wrong that has been done to us. He clothes us in his righteousness and makes us children of God.

A young woman who had been the victim of sexual abuse used to scrub herself in the bath with a scouring pad normally used to clean dirty pots. It was her attempt to get rid of the stain in her soul. Friends of mine met her, talked with her, wept with her, took her to the psalms of lament and took her to the cross. One day she bought a cloth—she no longer needed a scouring pad. It was a beautiful sign of her faith that Jesus truly cleanses us.

At the beginning of his ministry Jesus quoted from the opening of Isaiah 61 (Luke 4:18-21) and then claimed to be the One who fulfils it. This is what Isaiah 61 says:

> The Spirit of the Sovereign LORD is on me,
>> because the Lord has anointed me
>> to proclaim good news to the poor.
> He has sent me to bind up the broken-hearted ...
>> to comfort all who mourn,
>> and provide for those who grieve in **Zion** –
> to bestow on them a crown of beauty
>> instead of ashes,
> the oil of joy
>> instead of mourning,
> and a garment of praise
>> instead of a spirit of despair ...
> Instead of your shame
>> you will receive a double portion,
> and instead of disgrace
>> you will rejoice in your inheritance. (Isaiah 61:1, 3, 7)

"Where could I get rid of my disgrace?" asked Tamar. Like too many men over the years, Amnon refused to listen. But Jesus hears and he replies, "Instead of disgrace you will rejoice in your inheritance" (Isaiah 61:7). To women like Tamar, covered in ashes (2 Samuel **13:19**), Jesus promises "a crown of beauty instead of ashes" (Isaiah 61:3). Tamar was left "desolate" (2 Samuel **13:20**). Isaiah 61:4 uses the same word to describe "devastated" cities. But Jesus will "renew" what once was desolate and devastated. You can bring

> "Where could I get rid of my disgrace?" asks Tamar. The answer will be at the cross.

the shame that haunts your dreams and the disgrace you can't remove to Jesus. Tamar left weeping with her robe torn (2 Samuel **13:18-19**). Jesus promises "to bind up the broken-hearted" and clothe them with "a garment of praise instead of ... despair" (Isaiah 61:1, 3).

Questions for reflection

1. How strong is your moral authority? Is it compromised by your own weakness and sellout to sin in other areas of life?

2. *Bad parenting usually leads to wayward children.* How have you seen that in the lives of others or yourself? What can you take from this tragic story to encourage yourself or others?

3. What are you ashamed of? Perhaps things that you have done, or things that have been done to you? Bring them now to Jesus who has borne our shame and sorrow.

4. We are all used to morally compromised political leaders. How should this truth shape how we pray to our perfect King Jesus for them?

PART TWO

In **14:23-24** Absalom is restored and all is well. Or so it seems. At this point we're told that Absalom was "handsome" (**v 25**). You might suppose this to be a positive statement. But the same word (translated "beautiful") was used to describe Tamar in **13:1** and Tamar's beauty led to her destruction—although she herself was blameless. And Absalom's beauty will lead to his destruction—because of his culpable vanity. He has no external blemish (**14:25**). But his heart is another matter. In **verse 12** David told the woman of Tekoa, "not one hair of your son's head will fall to the ground." Here is yet another irony woven into the story. Not a hair of Absalom's head does fall to the ground, for each year he gathers up all his cut hair to weigh it (**v 26**). But it's a sign of vanity rather than his security, for it will lead to his untimely death. For now, he is quite literally preening himself for leadership (**v 26**).

Absalom has the looks and he has the ambition. But Samuel was told not to look at the outward appearance when anointing David as Saul's successor (1 Samuel 16:7). What kind of leader do you want? An outwardly impressive leader or someone with true character? When it comes to evangelism, do you want to point to prestige and power? Or are you content to preach the folly and weakness of the crucified King (1 Corinthians 1:18-25)?

Three sons and a daughter are born to Absalom (2 Samuel **14:27**). The sons are unnamed (possibly because they died in infancy, see 18:18). The daughter is called Tamar and, like her namesake, she is "beautiful" (**13:1**; **14:27**). Perhaps this is meant to indicate some measure of resolution to the story of Tamar.

But the story of Absalom himself is not resolved, for Absalom now begins his rise to power. When Joab refuses to give any further help (**v 28-29**), Absalom forces an encounter (**v 30-31**). As with the focus on his hair, it recalls the story of Samson (Judges 15:3-5), another man who contrived his own downfall. Absalom claims he is still in a de facto exile (2 Samuel **14:32**). So Joab mediates and Absalom is

restored to the court (**v 33**). Absalom calls David's bluff with an ulti-
matum: *accept me or execute me* (**v 32**). And he wins. David caves in.
Absalom is treated like a royal son again. His mind is on succession.

The Rebellion of Absalom

In the sixteenth century Niccolò Machiavelli wrote *The Prince*. It's a
cynical manual on gaining political power through everything from
diplomatic conceits to violent insurrection. Maybe Machiavelli got
a few ideas from Absalom. Certainly Absalom is a master at political scheming. First, Absalom ensures he looks like a king in waiting
(**15:1-2**). Second, he hints that he would speed up justice (**v 2-4**).
The genius of this tactic is that Absalom never actually has to make
any hard decisions. He can just go around implying that he would
decide in your favour. Everyone thinks he's on their side. Third, he
portrays himself as a man of the people (**v 5-6**). It all has a very contemporary ring to it. Absalom is the consummate political operator.
He's a spin-doctor's dream. The predictable outcome is that Absalom
"stole the hearts of the people of Israel" (**v 6**).

But there is a hint at Absalom's true intentions in the verb "take
hold" in **verse 5**. It's the same word used of Amnon taking hold of
Tamar to rape her in **13:11** (translated "grabbed" in the NIV). The king
was supposed to be a husband to the nation. But Absalom is bent on
national rape.

Absalom is patient for four years. But when the moment comes, he
moves with remarkable speed and without wavering (**15:7-9**). **Verse 7**
could instead refer to the 40th—and therefore final—year of David's
reign, perhaps at a point when Solomon has already been appointed
as David's successor (1 Kings 1:17). So this may be why Absalom acts
when he does.

Absalom lies to obtain the king's permission to hold a gathering at
Hebron, where in 2:1-4 David was first anointed king. Then Absalom
gathers leading figures in Israel to what is, in effect, his enthronement
(**15:10-12**). Some come willingly; some are tricked into attending,

making them complicit against their will (**v 11**). Before we can quite catch up with what's happening, David is fleeing from Jerusalem. David, the fugitive who became king, is a fugitive once again. But this time his own son is pursuing him. Jerusalem, the city of David, has become a city of danger.

Absalom's actions are evil. Not only is he a **Machiavellian** schemer, but he has rejected the LORD's anointed. Even when David had been anointed as the future king, he refused to rise against Saul. But Absalom has no regard for God's will. And yet he *fulfils* God's will. His actions are the culmination of God's word of

> God can use even people's evil actions to accomplish his purposes.

judgment against David (12:10-12). God can use even people's evil actions to accomplish his purposes (Genesis 50:20; Acts 2:23; 4:27-28 and Romans 8:28-30).

The Exile of David

It is as if the narrator describes David's departure from Jerusalem in slow motion. The civil war, when it comes, is described in 3 verses (2 Samuel 18:6-8). David's walk out of the city is described in 39 verses. This is because en route David encounters a series of people who must choose whose side they're on—just as we must choose whether to follow the crucified King or the latest brand of popularism (**15:13-18**).

1. Ittai

The Kerethites, Pelethites and Gittites are Philistines who have become David's followers (**v 18**). Most presumably joined David during his stay in Philistia. Ittai, however, is a recent recruit (**v 19-20**). Nevertheless, he commits himself to David—at the very moment when David looks to be a bad bet (**v 21-22**). The point is that these foreign "converts" to David's messiahship are more loyal than "the people of Israel" (**v 13**). It is another sign that God's plan of salvation is for the nations and that the true children of Abraham are those who share Abraham's faith. Today, too, we are asked to back the messiahship of Jesus when the majority are against him and his cause on earth looks weak. Our commitment to Christ makes us exiles (**v 19**; 1 Peter 1:1, 17; 2:11). And like Ittai, we are to commit to God's Messiah "whether it means life or death" (2 Samuel **15:21**; see Philippians 1:20).

2. Zadok and Abiathar

Once again an Israelite "king" pursues David (David calls Absalom the "King" in 2 Samuel **15:19**), and once again David retreats to the wilderness, both literally and **figuratively** (1 Samuel 23:14; 2 Samuel **15:23**, **28**; **16:2**). Five times in **15:22-23** the word "pass by" is used (translated in the NIV as "march on … marched on … passed by … crossed … moved on"). It's used elsewhere to describe Israel's **exodus** from Egypt (Exodus 15:16). But David is undergoing a kind of reverse exodus—an exile from home.

In 1 Samuel 4 the Israelites took the ark into battle, somewhat superstitiously hoping it would bring them success. But David knows his future does not depend on furniture, but on the favour of God. He commits his future to God (2 Samuel **15:24-26**). He recognises that God is punishing him (12:10). He is now in the hands of God's mercy. He adopts the posture of a penitent mourner (**15:30**). Not that this means David does not act. He sends Zadok and Abiathar back to be his spies in Jerusalem (**v 27-29**).

David was exiled from Jerusalem "up the Mount of Olives, weeping as he went" (**v 30**). Jesus would walk up the Mount of Olives weeping (Luke 19:37-44; 22:39-46) as he faced exile in our place. David was exiled for his own sins. Jesus would be exiled on the cross for our sins so we can escape the judgment of God.

3. Hushai

We find the same mix of faith and action in the next episode. As David climbs the Mount of Olives, he prays that God would thwart the advice of Ahithophel (2 Samuel **15:31**; 16:23). And then, at the place where God used to be worshipped, Hushai appears—the answer to David's prayer (**15:32**). So David sends Hushai to subvert the counsel of Ahithophel (**v 33-37**).

4. Ziba

Ziba, Mephibosheth's steward (see 2 Samuel 9), offers provisions (**16:1-2**). When David asks about Mephibosheth (who is presumably physically unable to join the "exodus"), Ziba claims Mephibosheth is disloyal (**v 3**). So David grants Ziba Mephibosheth's lands (**v 4**). At this point we are given no alternative to this account (that will come in 19:24-30). But we might wonder how likely it would be that Mephibosheth is thinking the ambitious, vain Absalom will ride into Jerusalem and promptly hand over the kingdom to a rival!

5. Shimei

The humiliation of David's reaches a climax with the arrival of Shimei, a member of Saul's family. Shimei rains down curses on David along with mud and stones (**16:5-6, 13**) Again, Shimei's words are laced with irony. He interprets David's fate as a punishment from God for his bloodguilt against the house of Saul (**v 7-8**). But the narrative of 1 and 2 Samuel has carefully exonerated David of any guilt in the deaths of Saul, Jonathan, Abner and Ish-Bosheth. Nevertheless, Shimei's words contain truth. "The LORD has given the kingdom into the hands of your son Absalom," he says in **verse 8**. "You have come to ruin because you are a murderer." This much is true. David *did* murder Uriah and his ruin is the fulfilment of Nathan's word in 12:9-10. So David recognises the voice of God in the curses of Shimei (**16:9-11**), even though Shimei's own intent is malicious (as David also recognises in

1 Kings 2:8-9). David is innocent of Saul's blood, but he's not inno-cent. What's happening is God's judgment. But therein lies David's confidence. God is not losing control, but fulfilling his word.

In 2 Samuel **16:13-14** David arrives at his "destination". Presum-ably this is his resting place for the night. But perhaps we should also read it symbolically. David's destination is the realisation of the previ-ous verse: "It may be that the LORD will look upon my misery and restore to me his covenant blessing instead of his curse today" (**v 12**).

> David leaves Jerusalem with everything—for he has God.

The original text is likely to be "look on my iniquity". Various alternatives have been introduced to smooth over the oddness of David claiming that God will look on his sin and do him good. But this is precisely the God Da-vid has come to know—a God who shows mercy to sinners (12:13).

God is fulfilling the word of the prophet Nathan in 12:9-10. But God gave David *another* word through Nathan: the promise of an eternal kingdom (7:11-16). These two words drive this narrative. Da-vid endures trouble because of the word of judgment in chapter 12. David has hope because of the word of promise in chapter 7.

Think back to the last time you couldn't sleep. What was the rea-son? Let's exclude wakeful children and physical illness. Think back to the last time you couldn't sleep because something was on your mind. What was it? Anxiety? Anger? Angst?

Psalm 3 is a psalm for us when we lie awake at night. It was writ-ten when David fled from Absalom. It begins, "LORD, how many are my foes! How many rise up against me!" (v 1) Perhaps David began composing it as he trudged along the road out of Jerusalem. Perhaps he thought of Shimei when he sang, "Many are saying of me, 'God will not deliver him.'" (Psalm 3:2)

We might think David would be full of anxiety, anger and angst.

We might imagine him lying awake on that first night, full of brooding and foreboding:

■ with anxiety about the future.

■ with anger about the present.

■ with angst about the past.

But in fact in verses 5-6 David says he can sleep well:

"I lie down and sleep;
    I wake again, because the Lord sustains me.
I will not fear though tens of thousands
    assail me on every side."

What's the secret? Verse 3 says: "You, LORD, are a shield around me, my glory, the One who lifts my head high" Normally a king's shield is his army. Most of David's army have deserted him. A king's glory is his palace, his court, his robes. David has left his palace and put on clothes of mourning. A king is lifted up on a throne. David is a long way from his throne. But David sleeps well because God himself is his shield and glory. In one sense David leaves Jerusalem with nothing. But in fact David leaves Jerusalem with everything—for he has God.

Remember this next time you lie awake with anxiety, anger or angst. God himself is your shield and glory.

■ The thing you're anxious about losing is no loss compared to God.

■ The thing you're angry about losing is no loss compared to God.

■ The guilt you feel is no guilt if your bring it to the cross to be forgiven and cleansed.

If God is your glory, then you can rejoice in any circumstance. And sleep well.

2 Samuel 13 v 1 - 16 v 14

Questions for reflection

1. Loyal friends are a gift and a blessing from God. Are there friends that you can be thankful to God for now? Do you need to show your faithfulness as a friend to someone else?

2. Spiteful enemies can humiliate and harass you, but they can never harm the real you—you are kept safe by God. How can you encourage yourself to trust in God's sovereignty when you are facing opposition?

3. Do you ever have trouble sleeping? Go through the points above, and work out how you can give your anxiety, anger or guilt to God.

8. THE FALL OF ABSALOM AND THE RISE OF DAVID

These chapters are all about a battle for control. At stake is who will be king in Israel. The contenders are Absalom and David. The outcome is a surprise.

Absalom reaches the height of his rise in **16:15-23**. In **verse 15** he enters the royal city with "all the men of Israel". And the first man Absalom meets declares, "Long live the king!" (**v 16**).

But all is not what it seems. The man is Hushai and we know he's loyal to David. Plus his words are highly ambiguous. Which king is he talking about? They appear to be a declaration of loyalty to Absalom, but to the reader they sound like defiance and accusation. Absalom is suspicious (**v 17**).

Again, Hushai's reply is ambiguous for he says he is loyal to "the one chosen by the LORD, by these people" (**v 18**). We know these are not the same person. Much of the story of Samuel has been about the tension between the king chosen by God (David) and the king chosen by the people (Saul and now Absalom). Finally, in **verse 19** Hushai says he will serve Absalom. But the reader knows Hushai's words are based on words suggested by David in 15:34. His pledge of loyalty to Absalom is in fact an act of obedience to David.

Who's in control? It looks like Absalom. But the first act of Absalom's regime is an act of obedience to David.

Ahithophel advises Absalom to sleep publicly with David's concubines (**16:20-22**). This was as much a political act as a sexual act (3:7-8). It was a declaration of Absalom's potency to reign. After this, there would be no going back. So it would lock in Absalom's current supporters (**16:21**). More significantly, it's the fulfilment of God's judgment against David in 12:11-12: "Before your very eyes I will take your wives and give them to one who is close to you, and he will sleep with your wives in broad daylight. You did it in secret, but I will do this thing in broad daylight before all Israel." The event takes place at the very spot where David's sin began in 11:2.

At this point the tide turns. As we've seen, two divine words drive this story: God's word of promise in 2 Samuel 7 and God's word of judgment in 2 Samuel 12. God's word of judgment has reached its fulfilment. Now his word of promise takes over.

Ahithophel's advice, we're told, was godlike (**16:23**). But his advice is subverted by Hushai. Ahithophel counsels an immediate attack to defeat David while he's weak (**17:1-4**). But Hushai, perhaps calculating the foolish option to be the opposite of whatever Ahithophel advises, counsels delay (**v 5-13**). Alluding to David's past as a renowned guerrilla fighter, Hushai says that any early losses would strike fear throughout Absalom's men (**v 7-10**). He flatters Absalom with the thought of leading a large army (**v 11-13**). In case Absalom changes his mind, Hushai dispatches David's pre-arranged messengers (**v 15-17**). In a story reminiscent of Rahab hiding the two spies (Joshua 2), they escape capture (2 Samuel **17:18-22**). God is with David just as he was with Joshua.

The reason Hushai's advice prevails is because "the LORD had determined to frustrate the good advice of Ahithophel in order to bring disaster on Absalom" (**v 14**). Absalom has the people, the army, the capital and the top advisors. But God is at work to restore David and that will make all the difference.

Who's in control? Absalom is making the decisions. But "in the LORD's hand the king's heart is a stream of water that he channels towards all who please him" (Proverbs 21:1).

But notice, too, the individuals who remain faithful to God's anointed despite the risks. They each contribute to a chain that God uses to fulfil his purposes: Hushai, Zadok and Abiathar (2 Samuel **17:15**), Jonathan and Ahimaaz (**v 17**), an unnamed servant girl (**v 17**), a man in Bahurim and his wife (**v 18**), and Shobi, Makir and Barzillai (**v 27-29**). Our actions can seem insignificant, but often God connects them with the actions of others like links in a chain to fulfil his purposes.

> Absalom has the people, the army, the capital and the top advisors. But God is at work to restore David—and that will make all the difference.

The tide is turning and the first person to spot this is Ahithophel. He is, after all, the most shrewd man in the kingdom. He realises that he's backed the wrong side and so he kills himself (**v 23**).

In 16:14 David and his men were "exhausted". The same word is used again in **17:29**. But now it explains the provision of food and equipment by David's supporters—provisions that will revive them (**v 27-29**).

Desperately Hanging On

In **17:24-26** and **18:1-2** the two armies muster. Then David's army routs "Israel", which is Absalom's army (**v 6-8**). Absalom's conscript army is no match for David's smaller, but professional army. Joab's tactics follow Ahithophel's advice, now turned against Absalom: a quick strike that isolates the leader. But the battle is described briefly. The narrator's interest (like David's) is elsewhere.

David doesn't march with his army because his men are concerned for his safety (**v 3-4**). Perhaps they wonder if he's still up to it. He was in bed last time they went to war (11:1-2). Also, as we've seen, 15:7 could refer to the 40th—and therefore final—year of David's life. Meanwhile David's concern is Absalom's safety (**17:5**). He makes the wholly unrealistic request that in the midst of the battle the troops "be gentle" with Absalom (**18:5**). They must fight him gently!

In the event Absalom's hair becomes his downfall. As he tries to escape a group of David's men, his hair is caught in a tree. In a comical but tragic moment, his mule continues, but he's left hanging (**v 9**; Deuteronomy 21:23). Mules were a royal mount, and so Absalom's kingship disappears from under him. No one is sure what to do next for they have all heard David's charge not to harm Absalom (2 Samuel **18:10-13**). But Joab has no scruples. When he thought it was expedient to reconcile David and Absalom he did so (14:1-24). Now he calculates that it's expedient to be rid of Absalom. So he plunges three javelins into Absalom's heart (**18:14**). It's literally three "sticks", which might explain why Absalom has to be finished off by Joab's men (**v 15**).

Absalom's rebellion ends in ignominy (**v 16**). The man famed for his beautiful hair is caught by his hair in a tree. The man with pretensions to lead armies dies alone. The man who built a monument for himself in the King's Valley (**v 18**) receives the burial of a traitor, which is what the pile of stones indicates (**v 17**; see Joshua 7:26; 8:29 and 10:27). Both Absalom and Ahithophel die hanging, but Ahithophel at least receives a proper burial (2 Samuel **17:23**).

Who's in control? Death and defeat are the fate of all those who who choose to rule their own lives in defiance of God's anointed. The warning of Psalm 2:10-12 is a warning for us all. But the invitation to find refuge in King Jesus is there for all as well.

"Now therefore, O kings, be wise;
      be warned, O rulers of the earth.
   Serve the Lord with fear,

and rejoice with trembling.
Kiss the Son,
    lest he be angry, and you perish in the way,
    for his wrath is quickly kindled.
Blessed are all who take refuge in him."

Mourning Victory

Ahimaaz, the priest's son, wants to take the news to David (2 Samuel **18:19**). But Joab knows what happens to people who think they can profit from conveying good news that David thinks is bad news (1:13-16; 4:9-12). So Joab sends a Cushite (a foreigner) instead (**18:20-21**). But Ahimaaz insists and outruns the Cushite (**v 22-27**). Ahimaaz proclaims victory (**v 28**). But David's concern is the fate of Absalom (**v 29**). Ahimaaz's opening word is *shalom*: "peace" (translated "All is well"). David literally responds, "Is *shalom* with the boy Ab-salom?" Absalom means "my father is peace". Ahimaaz fudges the issue (**v 29**) and it's left to the Cushite to inform David of Absalom's death (**v 30-32**).

David's men have won a great victory and David's response is, "O my son Absalom! My son, my son Absalom!" (**v 33**) It is a potent mix of love, grief, guilt and self-pity. The victorious army soon catch the mood and sneak into the city like an army returning in defeat (**19:1-4**). This is a bitter victory—mourned rather than celebrated. In 12:19-20 David refused to grieve for a dead son. Now he cannot be consoled. The difference is that David expected the former to rise again (12:23), but he harbours no such hopes for rebellious Absalom.

It's left to a pragmatist like Joab to salvage the situation before David, having won the battle, loses the nation. As Joab rightly points out, "You love those who hate you and hate those who love you. You have made it clear today that the commanders and their men mean nothing to you. I see that you would be pleased if Absalom were alive today and all of us were dead" (**19:5-6**). He makes David greet the men before the army disintegrates (**v 7-8**).

David grieves over a beloved son, but there is more to his grief.

Absalom died because of his sinful rebellion against God's anointed. But he also died because of David's sin. God graciously spared David's life, but decreed calamity for David's family. "If only I had died instead of you," he says (**18:33**). The whole incident cries out for a King who will bear our fate, die our death and take away our guilt.

The Return of the King

Absalom is dead, but the people hesitate (**19:9-10**). A national debate ensues. David is still in exile. What should be done? For the writer, however, the question is clear: "So why do you say nothing about bringing the king back?" (**v 10**). David gets things moving by persuading his own tribe, Judah, to take a lead (**v 11-12**). He appeases them by making Amasa, once Absalom's army commander, the new commander as an act of reconciliation (**v 13**). David had made a similar offer to Abner in chapter 3 and, remembering how that ended, the astute reader will have a sense of foreboding. With the nation back on side, David sets off for Jerusalem (**v 14-15**).

David's journey back to Jerusalem is a mirror image of his departure. Everything is reversed. A shameful retreat becomes a triumphant entry. Along the way David meets again some of the people he met during his exit (**v 15-18**).

Shimei

Shimei had cursed David as he left (16:5-13). Now he ingratiates himself (**19:18-20**). David shows clemency because "today I am king over Israel" (**v 21-23**). No executions are needed to establish his kingship. Whether Shimei's confession is sincere is doubtful. But his feigned loyalty finds its match in David's response. For the moment, David's response is governed by the reality of the political situation. After all, Shimei comes with a thousand Benjaminites whose support cannot be spurned (**v 16-17**). But at his death David's true response is revealed when he urges Solomon to execute Shimei (1 Kings 2:8-9).

Ziba

Ziba had told David that Mephibosheth had betrayed him, so David gave Mephibosheth's lands to Ziba (16:1-4). Now Mephibosheth proclaims his innocence (**19:24-28**). David is said to have the wisdom of an angel. But this appears ironic, for David, unsure who to believe, splits the land between them (**v 29**). Although occurring first, it's feels like a parody of Solomon's exemplary wise judgment (1 Kings 3). In the story of Absalom there are plenty of references to "wisdom" (13:3; 14:2, 20) and "advice" (15:31, 34; **16:20, 23; 17:7, 14, 23**) as well as to people with angelic or divine discernment (14:17, 20; **16:23; 19:27**). But true wisdom is in short supply (Proverbs 1:7; 1 Corinthians 1:18-25).

Mephibosheth

Mephibosheth's response is a model of loyalty to God's christ, then and now (**19:30**). He claims no rights before the king. His loyalty is the result of the king's unmerited kindness. He's not after reward or even vindication. His only concern is the king's honour. Is this true of your loyalty to Jesus Christ?

Barzillai

While Mephibosheth has nothing to offer David, Barzillai is a wealthy man who provided for David's needs (**16:27-29**). But like Mephibosheth, Barzillai is motivated not by personal reward, but by loyalty to God's anointed. David invites him to live with him in the palace (**19:31-33**). But Barzillai says he's too old to enjoy its pleasures (**v 34-36**). Instead he sends his servant (perhaps his son) as a token of his support (**v 37-39**).

The Suffering Christ

The story of David played a significant role in the **apologetics** of the first Christians. There was a big credibility gap in their central claim that Jesus was God's promised king, for Jesus had lived his life on the margins with no palace and no army. Most damning of all, his life ended in defeat and execution. How could anyone seriously think Jesus was the Christ?

But on the road to Emmaus, the risen Jesus claims the disciples should have realised the Christ would suffer. The whole Old Testament is about Jesus and his sufferings (Luke 24:25-27, 44-47). In chapter 10 of *1 Samuel for You* we saw that the story of David was a key piece of that evidence. The trajectory of the life of Israel's greatest king was suffering followed by glory. He lived for years in the wilderness before becoming king. Now that pattern has been repeated within his reign. Once again David has been forced into the wilderness (15:23, 28; 16:2). He's been betrayed by those close to him. David is the suffering king who is ultimately victorious. So the sufferings of Jesus should have been no surprise to those who knew the story of David. 1 Peter 1:10-11 says that through the prophets (and Samuel is part of the "former prophets" in the Hebrew **canon**) the Spirit "predicted the sufferings of the Messiah and the glories that would follow." 2 Samuel chapters 13 – 16 are part of the proof that the suffering Christ is the true Christ.

> If the suffering Christ is the true Christ, then his suffering followers are true followers.

If the suffering Christ is the true Christ, then his suffering followers are true followers. Like Ittai, Zadok and Abiathar, Hushai, Ziba and Mephibosheth, Shimei and Barzillai, we encounter Christ when his cause is weak and despised. On earth we see him humbled and crucified. We see his followers mocked and ignored. So it's tempting to disassociate ourselves from him or keep our heads down. But the story of David's humiliation and restoration reminds us of the humiliation and exaltation of Jesus. The true King suffered to redeem his people and delays his glory to create an opportunity for repentance. So his sufferings confirm rather than undermine his claims. Meanwhile Jesus says, "If anyone is ashamed of me and my words in this adulterous and sinful generation, the Son of Man will be ashamed of them when he comes in his Father's glory with the holy angels" (Mark 8:38).

Questions for reflection

1. *Who is in control?* In what situations do you find it hard to believe that God is sovereign over the world, your work, your family, or your life?

2. Review the reconciliations of Ziba, Shimei and Mephibosheth with David. How might our faith and devotion to Christ sometimes be similar to theirs?

3. How might you use this story to warn those who oppose God's King, and to urge them to "kiss the Son" and take refuge in him?

PART TWO

A Share in the Christ

Just when it looks as if peace is being restored, the men of Judah and Israel start arguing over the honour of accompanying the king (**19:40-43**). In **verses 9-10** everyone hesitated to affirm David as king. Now the men of Israel get angry because the men of Judah didn't wait for them, and the men of Judah are outraged. Sheba—whom the writer calls "a troublemaker"—seizes the opportunity to start a rebellion (**20:1-2**). The "ten shares" in **19:43** is probably a reference to the ten northern tribes of Israel. But the "ten shares" quickly dissolve into "no share" (**20:1**)!

The section is almost wearying. Here we are *again*. Another rebellion against God's anointed. But this is the human story—a story of ongoing rebellion against God. Why would we expect anything different?

David tells Amasa, his new army commander, to muster the troops and meet him in three days' time (**v 4**). But Amasa takes longer (**v 5**). So David tells Abishai (Joab's brother) to lead the elite guard out against Sheba (**v 6-7**). Joab has just been replaced by Amasa (**19:13**). Now it's Joab's brother who is told to lead the men. But there's no doubt where the real power lies, for in **20:7** they're described as "Joab's men". Even David's reference to "your master's men" in **verse 6** is ambiguous. Is Abishai's master David or Joab?

Was Amasa's delay incompetence or disloyalty? We can't be sure. But the ambiguity is enough for Joab to regain control. They meet en route. As Joab approaches Amasa, Joab's dagger drops to the floor and Joab has to pick it up (**v 8**). Though we're not told this, it seems deliberate. Had Joab rushed towards Amasa with dagger drawn, Amasa would have defended himself. Instead Joab leans in to greet Amasa with a kiss and stabs him with the dagger that "happens" to be in his hand (**v 9-10**). Like King Eglon, Amasa doesn't suspect a dagger in the belly from the left hand (Judges 3:15-21). Once again we see Joab in all his ambiguity: fiercely loyal to David yet violently disobedient. Joab and Abishai continue on against Sheba.

Maybe you've been in a traffic jam because the cars in front are slowly down to look at an accident on the opposite side of the road. "Rubber-necking" it's called. Something like this is going on here. In a very human touch, the troops are slowing down to gawk at Amasa's body. So it has to be dragged away and covered (**v 11-13**).

The phrases "all the men of Israel" and "all the tribes of Israel" in **verses 2** and **14** are either **hyperbole** or evidence that Sheba's support quickly melts away once Joab-the-warlord is after him. Sheba is left besieged in the city of Abel Beth Maakah (**v 14-15**). "A wise woman" shouts to Joab from the city. Her bravado in front of Israel's hard-man is impressive. She proclaims the city's heritage and faithfulness (**v 16-19**). To attack would be to "destroy … a mother in Israel" and "swallow up the LORD's inheritance" (**v 19**). So a deal is struck: Sheba for the city. And Sheba's head duly comes flying over the city wall (**v 20-22**). The rebellion is over. David's officials are listed, a sign (as it was in 8:15-18) that order is restored (**20:23-26**).

The fate of Sheba mirrors the fate of Abimelek, whose story in Judges 9 has often hovered in the background of 1 and 2 Samuel. Abimelek was the archetypal self-appointed king who created only trouble—a kind of anti-king. Abimelek died when a woman dropped a stone on his head from a tower. Now Sheba dies when a woman arranges to have his head thrown from the fortress. Deadly women, deadly head wounds and objects thrown from fortresses are the common elements.

Abimelek's rebellion was satirised by Jotham, who caricatured him as a thorn-bush which anoints itself king of the trees (Judges 9:7-15). In his final words in 2 Samuel 23:6-7 David says:

"But evil men are all to be cast aside like thorns,
    which are not gathered with the hand.
Whoever touches thorns

> uses a tool of iron or the shaft of a spear;
> they are burned up where they lie."

Abimelek and Sheba are thorns. They can't be dealt with "with the hand". They require "a tool of iron or the shaft of a spear". In Numbers 33:55 God had warned his people that "if you do not drive out the inhabitants of the land, those you allow to remain will become barbs in your eyes and thorns in your sides". (See also Judges 2:1-3, 20-23.) But the thorns of Judges 9 and 2 Samuel 20 are not outsiders. Israel is producing its own thorn-bushes. So Micah 7 likens Israel to a harvest field that has not produced fruit. Instead "the best of them is like a brier, the most upright worse than a thorn hedge" (7:4). Isaiah warns, "The Light of Israel will become a fire, their Holy One a flame; in a single day it will burn and consume his thorns and his briers." (10:17; see also 33:10-12) It's a warning echoed in Hebrews 6:7-8.

But God also promises that through his suffering Servant "instead of the thorn-bush will grow the juniper, and instead of briers the myrtle will grow" (Isaiah 55:13). The home of God's people will no longer be plagued by thorns, literal or metaphorical (Ezekiel 28:24). When God's ultimate King, King Jesus, reigns, all the "thorny problems" that afflict God's people will be utterly consumed with fire (2 Samuel 23:7).

Who is in Control?

At the end of the story *who is in control?* Is it David or Absalom? Here's the surprise. In many ways the answer is Joab. David is on the throne, but he's been largely passive throughout the story. It was Joab who rehabilitated Absalom in chapter 14 and it was Joab who executed him in **18:14-15**. One of the few decisive things David did was to initiate the reconciliation of Judah and Israel by offering to make Amasa the army commander (**19:13**). But within days Joab murdered Amasa and regained control of the army (**20:8-10**). One of Joab's men cries, "Whoever favours Joab, and whoever is for David, let him follow Joab!" (**20:11**) It's another desperately ambiguous statement. Twice in the story David cries out, "What does this have to do with you?"

(16:10; **19:22**) or "What have I to do with you, you sons of Zeruiah?" (ESV), Joab and Abishai were sons of Zeruiah, David's sister. These are statements of disassociation. Joab and Abishai are not under David's control. Back in 3:39 David said the

> There are three certainties in life: death and taxes and God's word.

sons of Zeruiah were too powerful for him to act against them. And then the story ends: "Joab was over Israel's entire army" (**20:23**). David's on the throne, but he cannot reign without Joab and, when it suits him, Joab ignores David's commands.

So is Joab in control? Not entirely—as will become clear in 1 Kings 2:5-6, 28-35. And if 15:7 refers to the 40th year of David's reign, then the events of 1 Kings 2 take place within a year of the events of 2 Samuel 20.

David is on the throne. But his rule is curtailed. Not only that, much of the blessing of chapters 7 – 8 is lost by chapter 20. The Davidic dynasty turns out to be flawed like the Saulite dynasty. At the end of Judges rape and civil war were the marks of national decline. Now they are repeated in a sequence of stories which are full of echoes of Judges. The fate of Sheba—with its parallels to Judges 9—is the climax of this **motif**.

How do we live in a world that is out of control? Where is certainty to be found?

1. God's Word

It's often said that the only certainties in life are death and taxes. But Christians need to add a third certainty—death and taxes and *God's word*. As we've seen, two divine words drive this story. God's word of judgment in 2 Samuel 12 leads to David's humiliation. But as soon as that word is fulfilled, the tide turns. And what then drives the story is the second word of God to David: the word of promise in 2 Samuel 7.

Hushai's advice prevails because "the LORD had determined to frustrate the good advice of Ahithophel in order to bring disaster on Absalom" (**17:14**). It looks as if Ahithophel's godlike advice will be what shapes history (**16:23**). But Ahithophel is not God and he doesn't shape history. In 16:12 David saw God's hand in his downfall. But once God's word of judgment has been fulfilled (12:11-12; **16:20-22**), God's hand works against Absalom.

A host of characters have peopled this story. Some loyal to God's anointed; others treacherous. Others, like Joab, ambiguous. The flaws of David himself have been exposed. Who can we trust? Where is the certainty in the account? The answer is: in God and his covenant word. It's God's word that governs events.

It's the same today. We, too, live in an ambiguous world with ambiguous people. But God's word is utterly certain. When your life feels out of control, grasp hold of the promises of God because they won't budge. They'll be like an anchor that holds you safe in the storms of life.

2. God's King

What is the certain word that drives this story and the story of Jesus and our story? It's the promise of 2 Samuel 7 that God's King will reign over God's people for ever.

Why is this good news in an uncertain world? There's a clue in an aside to the story of Sheba's rebellion. **20:3** is dropped into the narrative with no apparent connection to what's going on around it.

"When David returned to his palace in Jerusalem, he took the ten concubines he had left to take care of the palace and put them in a house under guard. He provided for them but had no sexual relations with them. They were kept in confinement till the day of their death, living as widows."

These are the concubines with whom Absalom had slept to proclaim his power (**16:20-22**). It was a sign that he had grabbed the throne just as Amnon had "grabbed" Tamar (13:11). David's actions in **20:3** are ambiguous. He "provided" for them. But they are placed "under guard" and confined, living as "widows".

The key is the repetition of the number "ten" in **19:43** and **20:3**. The ten widows are intended to mirror the ten northern tribes of Israel. In **19:43** the men of Israel say, "We have ten shares in the king". But in the very next verse they rebel with the cry, "We have no share in David" (**20:1**). To reject God's king is to be left like a widow. But to embrace God's king is to embrace a husband. So Ephesians 5:25-27 talks about Jesus as:

- a husband who gives himself up for his bride.

- a husband who washes his bride clean through his word.

- a husband who promises to present her to himself as a radiant bride.

When life is out of your control, comfort yourself with this.

- *In the past Jesus gave his life for you.* His love is certain for he has demonstrated it at the cross.

- *In the present Jesus is at work in you.* As you view the circumstances of your life (those out-of-control circumstances) through the interpretative grid of his word, so Jesus uses those circumstances to make you holy.

- *In the future Jesus will make you radiant.* Life now may bring you down. You may feel fragile. You may feel crushed. But one day Jesus will lift you up to stand in his presence, holy and blameless.

That's his promise and his word is certain.

Questions for reflection

1. *"In the past Jesus gave his life for you."* Think about Jesus' death on the cross for you. Reflect on the strength and power of that unflinching, committed love towards you. How will you draw from it strength and courage for today?

2. *"In the present Jesus is at work in you."* What signs do you see of that? Some of them may be hidden or invisible to you. Ask a close friend to share their thoughts about how they see Jesus at work in your life now.

3. *"In the future Jesus will make you radiant."* Are you living just for today, or is your hope firmly set on the future, when we will be transformed, and all things shall be made new?

9. THE LORD IS MY ROCK

The final four chapters of Samuel are arranged in a chiastic structure—which explains some of the repetition in the storytelling:

a. Famine caused by Saul (21:1-14)

    b. David's mighty warriors (21:15-22)

        c. David's final song (**22:1-51**)

        c*. David's final words (**23:1-7**)

    b*. David's mighty warriors (23:8-39)

a*. Plague caused by David (24:1-25)

We'll work from the centre outwards.

A couple of years ago I was swimming in the sea in Scotland and found myself tiring. But, when I put my feet down to rest, there was nothing there. I was out of my depth. So I started to swim towards the shore. But I was being moved around in the swell. There was no strength in my limbs. I started feeling cold—which is a bad sign. I thought, "This is serious. I could drown here." Of course, I didn't shout for help because I am, after all, a man.

Then finally I felt solid ground under my feet. In that moment I knew I was safe. I was still in the water and still being pushed around by the waves. It was still a struggle to get to shore. But at any point I could put my feet down and feel solid ground.

Perhaps you feel as if the waves of life are overwhelming you. You may feel out of your depth. You may feel you're drowning under the pressures. They might be anxiety, loss or guilt. Maybe you can't give them a name. But you're struggling to cope. 2 Samuel 22 (and Psalm 18, where this song is repeated) is an invitation to put your feet down and feel firm ground underneath you as, by faith you rest on God the Rock.

2 Samuel 22 is David's reflection on his life (**v 1**). It gives us a way of reading history and a way of understanding what's happening in our lives. This is how the song opens:

> "The LORD is my rock, my fortress and my deliverer;
>> my God is my rock, in whom I take refuge,
>> my shield and the horn of my salvation.
> He is my stronghold, my refuge and my saviour—
>> from violent men you save me." (**v 2-3**)

The repeated word is "my", but this is not about David. This is David saying, *The LORD is everything to me. Throughout my life it has always been God who has protected me and saved me.*

"The Lord is my rock" is the "refrain" of this song. Not only does it open the song, but it's repeated in the middle and towards the end:

> "For who is God besides but the LORD?
>> And who is the Rock except our God?" (**v 32**)

> "The LORD lives! Praise be to my Rock!
>> Exalted be my God, the Rock, my Saviour." (**v 47**)

David's final words in 2 Samuel **23:3** also speak of God as "the Rock of Israel". *The LORD is my Rock*. What exactly does that mean?

God the Rock is Mighty to Save

David's life wasn't easy. Remember the writer of Samuel spends 20 chapters describing David's life after he becomes king in 2 Samuel 5, but he also spends 20 chapters describing David's life *before* he becomes king. His struggles are as important as his reign:

> "The waves of death swirled about me;
>> the torrents of destruction overwhelmed me.

The cords of the grave coiled around me;

the snares of death confronted me." (**22:5-6**)

The word "grave" is *Sheol*, the word for the afterlife or hell. It may be a pun, for *she'ol* sounds a bit like *sha'ul*, the word for Saul, and there were many times when David felt as if Saul was ensnaring him. There were times when David felt overwhelmed, as if he were being dragged into hell. But this is what David has learnt: "The LORD is my rock, my fortress and my deliverer" (**v 2**).

2 Samuel 21 and 23 list David's top soldiers. In 23:8 they're called "David's mighty warriors". When you read their exploits, you realise that they were hard men. Yet even with his mighty men around him, David's enemies were too strong for him. **22:18** says: "He rescued me from my powerful enemy, from my foes, who were too strong for me". David's saying that without these men he wouldn't be where he is today. But ultimately it's the LORD who's saved him from his enemies (**v 4**). The acknowledgment that really matters is, "The LORD is my Rock."

> In the end, the only dependable thing in life is God. He is our Rock.

In the end, the only dependable thing in life is God. He is our Rock. When our enemies are too strong for us, he's the one who is mighty to save. In **verses 7-15** God comes to David's aid. It's a powerful description of the power of God—a description that uses the language of Israel's encounter with God at Sinai.

The thundering of God also recalls his thundering against the Philistines in 1 Samuel 7:10. Hannah, too, promised, "The Most High will thunder from heaven" (1 Samuel 2:10). What has happened throughout the story of 1 and 2 Samuel is a repetition or continuation of the exodus. See the parallels in the table over the page.

2 Samuel **22:16** certainly continues with an exodus-like experience: "The valleys of the sea were exposed and the foundations of the earth

laid bare at the rebuke of the LORD, at the blast of breath from his nostrils." Just as happened in Exodus 14, a mighty wind—direct from the nostrils of God—blows on the waters, creating a valley through the sea and revealing the foundations of the earth beneath.

David is describing the exodus in these verses. He's not exaggerating for effect. He's describing something that really happened in history—the exodus from Egypt, the encounter at Sinai, the parting of the Red Sea. Except that it wasn't something that happened to *David* himself—not in the sense that he was there at the time. He was born hundreds of years later.

And yet in a very real sense it *did* happen to him. It happened *for* him. The freedom he enjoyed, the relationship with God, his identity as God's king were all founded on the exodus. That was the moment God liberated Israel and made them his people.

In that moment at the Red Sea, David was drawn out of the waters because Israel was drawn out of the waters (2 Samuel **22:17**). He was rescued from his enemies (**v 18-19**) and brought into a spacious place (**v 20**). He lived in the land because of that moment. And every deliverance David experienced—and there were many—was based on that great deliverance. David is saying, *Whenever I felt overwhelmed by life or entangled by death, I would look back to the exodus. I would confront my feelings with the fact of the exodus. God has created his people and he will not abandon his promises.*

The exodus was the great saving event that defined the identity of Israel. For us it's the resurrection of Jesus (to which the exodus and Passover pointed). Remember that David the christ is a pointer to Jesus the Christ. The song ends, "He gives his king great victories; he shows unfailing kindness to his anointed, to David and his descendants for ever" (**v 51**). David's experience would be the experience of Jesus. **Verses 5-7 and 17** describe a death and resurrection experience. Jesus would experience hell on the cross, but God would deliver him. Jesus would be overwhelmed by death, but God would raise him up to new life. And we are in Christ. Even though we weren't there at

2 Samuel 22	Exodus 19 – 20
The earth *trembled* and quaked, the foundations of the heavens shook; they trembled because he was angry (**v 8**).	The whole mountain trembled violently (19:18).
Smoke rose from his nostrils; consuming fire came from his mouth, burning coals blazed out of it (**v 9**).	Mount Sinai was covered with smoke, because the LORD descended on it in fire. The smoke billowed up from it like smoke from a furnace (19:18).
He parted the heavens and came down; *dark clouds* were under his feet … He made *darkness* his canopy around him—the *dark* rain clouds of the sky (**v 10-12**).	… with a thick *cloud* over the mountain … Moses approached the thick *darkness* where God was (19:16; 20:21)
Out of the brightness of his presence bolts of lightning blazed forth. The LORD thundered from heaven; the voice of the Most High resounded. He shot his arrows and scattered the enemy, with great bolts of lightning he routed them (**v 13-15**).	On the morning of the third day there was thunder and lightning (19:16). When the people saw the thunder and lightning and heard the trumpet and saw the mountain in smoke, they trembled with fear (20:18).

the time (as David was not at the exodus), *Jesus'* experience becomes *our* experience. God intervenes in our lives with resurrection power.

So you can say, in words similar to those of David, "Whenever I feel overwhelmed by life or entangled by death, I can look to the resurrection of Jesus. I can confront my *feelings* with the *fact* of the resurrection. *That's* the sign that God will recreate his people and will not abandon his promises."

David himself didn't feel the earth shake at Mount Sinai or hear the thunder or see the lightning or smell the smoke. But he realised that his experiences were an echo of Sinai. David didn't just get lucky with his slingshot when he faced Goliath. God intervened on his behalf. David didn't just get lucky when he escaped Saul. God intervened on his behalf. And when God intervenes on *your* behalf in your life it might look like the help of another Christian or a timely "coincidence". But David wants us to recognise it as an act of the earth-shaking, fire-breathing, darkness-dispelling God.

Let your imagination run riot! The next coincidence, the next illness cured by a doctor, the next timely word from a friend—see behind these things the God of the exodus and the God of resurrection. This is how to read history and understand your life.

- Next time you want to say, "I was struck by something I read in my Bible," instead say, "Jesus spoke to me through his word".

- Instead of saying, "A weird thing happened to me today," say, "The Father reached down into my life to provide a great opportunity for me".

- Instead of saying, "I don't know how I got through it," say, "The Spirit helped me with resurrection power".

My friend Matt's daughter was recently in hospital with brain cancer. Inevitably that created a **maelstrom** of emotions for him as a father. He once told me, "I wanted to rip a soap-dispenser off the wall today and smash it up. I don't know what stopped me." And I could say, "I know: it was the Holy Spirit helping you with resurrection power'.

Questions for reflection

1. "God is my Rock." When are you most vulnerable to not believing this truth? What experiences have you had as a Christian that confirm the truth of this statement?

2. Do you understand that God is at work in your life moment by moment? Reflect on things that have happened to you this week, and give thanks to God for his work in your life: to speak to you; to guide you; to strengthen you; to protect you.

3. How do you feel about using the language of God's involvement in your life highlighted at the end of this chapter? Are there dangers with talking like this? How can we encourage ourselves to speak more like this to others?

PART TWO

God the Rock Makes Us Mighty to Serve

Part one of this song shows how God the Rock is mighty to save. The second half starts in **22:31-32** with another reference to God as our Rock, and goes on to describe how God makes David mighty to rule. His feet do not give way (**v 34**). He has pursued, crushed, humbled and destroyed his enemies (**v 38-43**). Why? Because of God. "It is God who arms me with strength" (**v 33**).

"Your help has made me great," says David in **verse 36**. David is not a self-made man. He did not pull himself out of obscurity. It is God who has made him great (**v 17-20**). 1 Samuel 2:9 says, "Not by might shall a man prevail" (ESV). David refused to the seize the throne. But the throne became his because God gave it to him. Throughout the rebellion of Absalom he was weak and passive. But Absalom is dead and David is ending his life on the throne.

The agenda for 1 and 2 Samuel was set by Hannah's song. She sang, "The LORD ... humbles and he exalts" (1 Samuel 2:7). Now David makes the same reflection: "You save the humble, but your eyes are on the haughty [literally "the high"] to bring them low" (2 Samuel **22:28**). "He is the God who ... puts the nations under me ... You exalted me above my foes" (**v 48-49**). "Haughty" in **verse 28** and "exalted" in **verse 49** are the same word: God has brought down "the high" and "lifted high" David.

As we've noted, the distinguishing physical feature of Saul was that he was a head taller than anyone else. But the "high one" has been brought low and "little David" has been raised high in his place. When David lamented the death of Saul, his refrain was, "How the mighty have fallen" (1:19, 25, 27). Some versions of **22:36** read "You stoop down to make me great" (see NIV footnote). It's not just that God has brought Saul down and lifted David up. God himself has stooped low to lift David high.

According to **verse 44**, God not only delivered David "from the attacks of the peoples"; he also placed him over foreign nations: "People I did not know now serve me." David continues in **verses 45-46**:

"Foreigners cower before me;
    as soon as they hear of me, they obey me.
 They all lose heart;
    they come trembling from their strongholds."

God "puts the nations under" the authority of David (**v 48, 50**). This is a pointer to the authority of the risen Christ over all nations. God has made Jesus Lord over all nations. Jesus stooped low. "He humbled himself by becoming obedient to death—even death on a cross! Therefore God exalted him to the highest place and gave him the name that is above every name" (Philippians 2:8-9).

> God does not just call you to serve him; he also empowers you to serve him.

So in one sense this psalm is not about you. As the final verses make clear, this psalm is about Christ (2 Samuel **22:51**). But if you're *in* Christ and with Christ, then you share his authority. This psalm is being fulfilled today through the mission of the church. The kingdom of Christ is extended as we proclaim the word of Christ. Through our evangelism Christ is being made "the head of nations" (**v 44**; see Revelation 2:27-29).

How will we do that? How will we face hostility? 2 Samuel **22:33** says, "It is God who arms me with strength and keeps my way secure". What is it that you feel you cannot do? God does not just call you to serve him; he also empowers you to serve him. He gives all you need to do all he asks. The LORD the Rock arms you, keeps you, trains you, helps you, provides for you, strengthens you, delivers you and preserves you (**v 33, 35, 36, 37, 40, 44**). So we say in **verse 47**, "The LORD lives! Praise be to my Rock! Exalted be my God, the Rock, my Saviour!"

God the Rock Makes Us Righteous in Christ

So the first half of this song describes how God was mighty to save David. The second half describes how God makes *us* mighty to save. It all revolves around the central verses: **21-30**. Here David claims to be guiltless and blameless (**v 22-24**), and that God will reward him accordingly (**v 25-30**). "The LORD has dealt with me according to my righteousness," he says (**v 21**). "The LORD has rewarded me according to my righteousness" (**v 25**).

At this point you might be saying, "Hang on a minute. Isn't this the David who committed adultery and murder? If David is rewarded according to his righteousness, then surely he's in big trouble! How can he say this?" God "sets me free from my enemies," says David in **verse 49** and **verses 38-43**. But what if *God* is your enemy?

Part of the answer is that David is declaring God's *covenant* faithfulness. David uses similar language in Psalm 7:8. Psalm 7:12 goes on, "If a man does not repent, God will **whet** his sword" (ESV). The implication is that if you *do* repent, then your righteousness within the covenant is restored. So David is righteous in the same way that Abraham believed and it was credited to him as righteousness. Paul connects Abraham's and David's experience in this way in Romans 4:1-8. So David isn't claiming to be *sinless*, but to be *righteous*. And being righteous means having a right standing within the covenant—a covenant which included provision for sin through the sacrificial system. After the incident with Bathsheba, Nathan says to him, "The LORD has taken away your sin. You are not going to die" (2 Samuel 12:13).

So God blesses David because God overlooks David's sins. But how can God do this? The answer brings us back to the refrain of the song: *the LORD is my Rock*. Something of what this means is self-evident. God is firm, reliable, solid. We can depend on him. He provides a foundation for our lives (Matthew 7:24-27). But two stories show us why David makes *this* the refrain of his song and—since David is looking back in this song—the refrain of his whole life. This was the soundtrack of his life: the LORD is my Rock.

Story 1: The Rock of Parting

In 1 Samuel 23 King Saul is trying to kill David. Saul is going along one side of a mountain; David is hurrying on the other side. It seems a bit Tom-and-Jerry—backwards and forwards. Then the Philistines attack and Saul has to abandon the chase. That mountain is simply referred to as "the rock" (1 Samuel 23:25). David is protected by "the rock". The rock comes between him and Saul. It becomes known as "the rock of parting" because it keeps David apart from his enemies.

Now at the end of his life David says, "Who is the Rock?" (2 Samuel **22:31**). "The Lord is my rock." All along God has been like that rock-mountain. God stands between us and our enemies. As death and judgment approach, God himself interposes himself in the person of his Son. Jesus stands between us and our enemies. He absorbs the full force of divine wrath. As a result, he becomes "my rock, my fortress and my deliverer" (**v 2**).

Story 2: The Rock is Christ

David is not the first person in the Bible to call God "the Rock". Moses also sang a song at the end of his life to reflect on his days with exactly the same refrain: *the Lord is my Rock.* He mentions it six times (Deuteronomy 32:4, 15, 18, 30, 31, 36-37). This reflects a defining moment in the life of Moses. Soon after God rescued Israel out of slavery, the people complained. They were testing God—putting God on trial. *What would God do?*

The Israelites have put God on trial through their grumbling. And so God arranges a courtroom. The **choreography** is significant. The representatives of Israel are on one side (Exodus 17:5). God says, "I will stand there before you by the rock at Horeb" (v 6). So God is on the other side. This is the case of "Israel *versus* God". In the middle is Moses with his staff, and God specifically says that this is the staff that brought judgment on Egypt (v 5). So Moses is, so to speak, the judge. All this takes place "in front of the people" so everyone can see what happens (v 5).

We know the Israelites are guilty and deserve to be condemned. We know God is innocent and deserves to be vindicated. But God tells Moses, "Strike the rock" (v 6). Moses brings down the rod of judgment *on God*. God takes the judgment that his people deserve. As a result blessing flows to the people. In this case it literally flows for water comes out from the rock to quench the people's thirst (v 6).

Paul says, "That rock was Christ" (1 Corinthians 10:4). "For they drank from the spiritual rock that accompanied them, and that rock was Christ." The story was a picture of, and pointer to, the cross. At the cross the great court case between God and humanity comes to its climax. On one side is

> At the cross the great court case between God and humanity comes to its climax.

guilty humanity—you and I—deserving condemnation. On the other side is the perfect, sinless Son of God, Christ the Rock. And God the Father says, "Strike the rock". The rod of his judgment falls on Jesus.

So when Moses calls God "the Rock" and when David calls God "the Rock", they mean that God is the Rock who takes our judgment on himself.

This song is not a challenge to achieve. Christ has achieved everything for us. David's message to us is this: *There is a Rock on which you can stand. If you put your feet on that Rock, then you can keep your head above water.*

Stop swimming. Take a moment to put your feet down. Feel solid ground underneath. God has dealt with your sin. And he will bring you safely to the shore. You may still be in the water and the waves may still throw you around. But there is a Rock beneath your feet. Stretch out your faith—as you might stretch out your feet when swimming—and feel it there. Stop trying to be your own saviour. Discover the truth that Christ is "my rock, my fortress and my deliverer" (2 Samuel **22:2**).

A King Like the Sun

2 Samuel 22 shows how God has created and sustained the rule of the Davidic king. But what is that rule like? In 2 Samuel **23:1-7** we have David's last words (**v 1**). They offer us David's theory of kingship. He likens a just king to the sun (**v 4**). This draws on Genesis 1:16: "God made two great lights—the greater light to govern the day and the lesser light to govern the night". The sun "governs" the day and a good king "governs" like the sun. Throughout the ancient world—and this is reflected in the Bible—rulers were likened to celestial bodies (and the deposing of rulers was likened to the falling of stars).

Specifically a good king brings light from darkness and plants from the earth (2 Samuel **23:4**). Again, there is an echo of Genesis 1, where light dispelled darkness and "the land produced vegetation" in response to God's word (Genesis 1:1-3, 11-12). Creation was then entrusted to humanity, which was given the task of ruling over creation to nurture and fill it. A just rule blesses the earth (see also Psalm 72).

Humanity's rebellion has warped our rule, so now it's partial and corrupt. One sign of this in Genesis 3 is that the land "will produce thorns and thistles for you". (Genesis 3:18). In 2 Samuel **23:6-7** we meet thorns, but here they are "evil men" who oppose the rule of God's king. David has had to deal with a few of these during his reign (see especially the comments on 2 Samuel 20). But under the just reign of God's king they are utterly "burned up". God's covenant with David was for all humanity. David's descendant will restore the rule of humanity, and through that restoration creation itself will be renewed (Romans 8:19-23).

At the heart of David's final words is this verse:

"If my house were not right with God,
    surely he would not have made with me an
    everlasting covenant,
    arranged and secured in every part;
  surely he would not bring to fruition my salvation
    and grant me my every desire." (2 Samuel **23:5**)

Is David's house right with God? If we had just read 2 Samuel 11 – 20, then we would conclude that it's not. But the key is the "everlasting covenant" (**23:5**). David's house is right with God not because it always acts in a right way. It does not. It's right with God because of God's covenant with David in chapter 7. David's descendants will not always rule "in righteousness" (**v 3**). But as Israel's kings failed, God's covenant with David would create the expectation of a coming son of David—a righteous One who would rule rightly. So **verses 2-4** become a beautiful prophecy that find their fulfilment (via Isaiah 61:1-2) in Luke 4:18-21. This king's reign would be like the sun, dispelling darkness and restoring creation.

Questions for reflection

1. *God the Rock makes us mighty to serve.* How are you engaged in serving at the moment: in your church; in your family; in your community?

2. *Righteous in Christ.* David, more than most, could look back on his life and see the appalling sins he had committed, and yet stand confident before a holy God. Do you have the same confidence through the cross of Christ?

3. *God is my rock.* Think about what gives you a sense of security and stability in life? Is it your relationships; your bank balance; your achievements; your job; your home? How can we give thanks to God for each of these, yet resist the temptation to make them ultimate things?

10. THE LORD IS MY SHEPHERD

As we saw in the previous chapter, the final four chapters of Samuel are arranged in a chiastic structure. In chapter nine we looked at the central sections (22:1-51 and 23:1-7). In this chapter we move outwards, looking first at David's mighty men in **21:15-22** and **23:8-39**.

David's Mighty Men

In 2 Samuel 21 the writer brings together four stories of four heroes linked by the common ancestry of their combatants (**v 22**). Their opponents are all descendants of "Rapha" or "the Rephaim" (**v 16, 18, 20, 22**) which itself means "giant".

- Abishai (**21:15-17**)

- Sibbekai (**21:18**)

- Elhanan (**21:19**)

- Jonathan (**21:20-22**)

In **verses 15-17** David is exhausted and Ishbi-Benob, a Philistine with a massive armoury, threatens to finish him off. Then Abishai intervenes to rescue David. David's army prevents him ever engaging in battle again—probably because he's getting old. He is God's anointed so they cannot risk losing him.

In the original Hebrew **verse 19** says that Elhanan killed Goliath, which appears to contradict the story of David killing Goliath in

1 Samuel 17. Several explanations have been suggested for this apparent discrepancy. Some suggest Elhanan is another name of David since he's from Bethlehem (though no other evidence exists for this). Others suggest this is the result of a copying error, and the original text said Elhanan killed "the brother of Goliath" (a suggestion reflected in the wording of the NIV).

The book of Samuel did not go to press after having been carefully proofread. The first edition was handwritten and subsequent editions were handwritten copies of copies. A few differences inevitably crept in. The text of these closing chapters is particularly difficult (as a comparison on English translations of chapter 23 will reveal). But in God's **providence** the differences don't affect any significant **doctrinal** issues. Certainly the parallel passage in 1 Chronicles 20:5 says, "Elhanan son of Jair killed Lahmi the brother of Goliath the Gittite".

In 2 Samuel **21:20-22** Jonathan defeats a man with 24 digits. Not only does this man threaten Israel, he also taunts Israel (just as Goliath had done in 1 Samuel 17:10, 25, 26, 36, 43-44). He brings dishonour to God—until Jonathan finishes him off.

2 Samuel **23:8-39** describes the hard men of David's army! They may seem like odd role models for contemporary Christians, but they, like us, are servants of the king. Moreover, the key principles are those established back at the beginning of 1 and 2 Samuel in Hannah's song: "There is no rock like our God." "The LORD ... brings low and he exalts." "Not by might shall man prevail." "The LORD will ... exalt the power of his anointed." (1 Samuel 2:2, 7, 9, 10 ESV)

The Named Three

We see these principles illustrated in the account of "the Three" (2 Samuel **23:8-12**). There's no doubt that the exploits of Josheb-Basshebeth, Eleazar and Shammah are impressive. They showed great prowess and courage, standing alone against the enemy. But we shouldn't miss the secret of their success: "The LORD brought about a great victory" (**v 10, 12**).

In Shakespeare's play *Macbeth*, Macbeth is told he will not be killed by one born of a woman. Safe in this knowledge, he lunges into battle without fear (until he discovers Macduff was born by caesarean section). We can enter the battle with the same fearlessness, safe in the knowledge that the victory belongs to the Lord.

The Unnamed Three

A passing expression of homesickness leads to a reckless raid to collect water from the heart of the enemy camp. David expresses a longing for water from Bethlehem's well. When three of his warriors risk their lives to collect some of this water, David appears to respond with callous indifference as he pours it on the ground. In fact David realises the true enormity of what's been done. The water represents the blood of his men and he's unworthy to drink it. Only the LORD is worthy of such devotion. Augustine and Ambrose both saw this as a warning against "uncontrolled desire" (*Confessions* 10.31.46-47 and *Jacob and the Happy Life* 1.1.3). When David sees the impact of his selfish longings on other people, he rededicates his desires to God.

The Thirty

The chapter ends with more heroes. With Abishai (**v 18-19**) and Benaiah (**v 20-23**) we get more stories of amazing courage. Most of these warriors just get an honourable mention—they are honoured in the pages of Scripture as they deserve to be. They fought for the kingdom. They brought rest to God's people (7:1). None were perfect, (Uriah's name at the end of the list reminds us that David's reign was hardly free from sin). No doubt they were rough, hard men—not your ideal dinner guests. But they were faithful to God's king. They earned their "Well done, good and faithful servant" (Matthew 25:21). They perhaps find a counterpart in the lists of names at the end of some of Paul's epistles, like Romans 16 and Colossians 4, where Paul honours those who served with him in the gospel.

The hard men of David's army:

- fought in the strength of God.

- were devoted to God's king.

- sought the honour of God.

How do you measure up to each of these criteria?

These are some of the heroes of David's reign and the writer duly honours them, giving each his full ancestral name. But there is more to this than a list of heroes. These verses illustrate David's supremacy over the Philistines. They demonstrate that God has fulfilled the promise he made in 2 Samuel 3:18, that David would rescue the people from Philistines. The true hero of the story is God himself. He has brought David to the throne and he has delivered Israel from her enemies.

> The true hero of the story is God himself. He has brought David to the throne and he has delivered Israel from her enemies.

The Censured Census

What's the worst ending to a book or movie you can think of? At first sight the ending of 1 and 2 Samuel is a contender. David's song in chapter 22, his last words in **23:1-7** and his mighty warriors in **23:8-39** all look like great endings to the story. But none of them are followed by the caption "The End". We still have one chapter to go and that chapter is something of an anti-climax. For one thing it describes an act of administration—a census. We find ourselves in the wonkish world of national statistics. Instead of ending with the exploits of warriors, we end with the exploits of civil servants. More significantly, instead of ending on a note of triumph, we end with failure.

What's more, this final story is almost certainly out of place in the chronology. This is not the last of the events described in 2 Samuel. The writer has chosen to put it at the end and make it the conclusion. Why?

The Brutality of Atonement

Before we explore 2 Samuel 24, we need to think about its counterpart in the chiastic structure of chapters 21 – 24. In chapter 21 there are three years of famine in the land as a result of sin committed by Saul. In chapter 24 there are three days of plague in the land as a result of sin committed by David (and three years of famine was an option according to **24:13**). In chapter 21 we are told that as a result of an act of "atonement" (**v 3**), "God answered prayer on behalf of the land" (**v 14**). The same phrase is used in chapter 24 when, after sacrifices are offered, "the LORD answered … prayer on behalf of the land" (**24:25**).

In 2 Samuel 21 there's famine in the land for three years. So David seeks God's face, and in response God explains that the famine is a judgment on a crime Saul committed against the Gibeonites (**v 1-3**). Back in Joshua 9 the Gibeonites tricked Israel into giving them protection, and so the Israelites swore never to kill them. But it seems that, in a fit of nationalist zeal, Saul had massacred some Gibeonites—an event not recorded in the Bible. The implication is profound. The LORD is not like other "nationalistic gods"—who only ever do good things to their people, and always oppose their enemies. The living God will not ignore the shedding of innocent blood—whoever it belongs to— nor the breaking of a covenant made in his name. Therefore he is punishing his own people for this crime with famine.

So David asks the Gibeonites how atonement can be made: "What shall I do for you? How shall I make atonement so that you will bless the LORD's inheritance?" (2 Samuel **21:3**) Atonement means "putting right". *How can things be put right between us? What needs to happen? What price needs to be paid?* One person has been wronged by another and atonement is the process of putting it right so reconciliation can take place.

The response of the Gibeonites can be understood in different ways. The ESV says: "It is not a matter of silver or gold between us and Saul or his house; neither is it for us to put any man to death in Israel" (**v 4**). In other words, *This requires more than monetary compensation. This requires the shedding of blood, but we don't have the right to execute anyone.* So David agrees to their request for seven male descendants of Saul to be executed (**v 5-9**).

In Numbers 35:33 God says:

"Do not pollute the land where you are. Bloodshed pollutes the land, and atonement cannot be made for the land on which blood has been shed, except by the blood of the one who shed it. Do not defile the land where you live and where I dwell, for I, the LORD, dwell among the Israelites."

Literally, Joshua 9 says Israel "cut" a covenant with the Gibeonites (Joshua 9:15-16). This is a graphic reference to the way that covenants were made. An animal was cut up and the pieces lined up in pairings of two halves. The covenant-makers then walked between the pieces to signify that if they broke the covenant, the same fate would befall them as befell the animal (Genesis 15). Now that fate would befall the house of Saul.

Deuteronomy 24:16 says children should not die for the sins of their fathers. But Saul's massacre was not simply an individual act by Saul. He was acting as the representative of his family and nation. Today, if a national leader commits an act of personal revenge, then he alone pays the consequences. But if he commits a crime in his capacity as a leader (for example, ordering the assassination of a foreign leader), then the consequences fall on the nation he represents. Ultimately this principle lies at the heart of our salvation, as Paul shows in Romans 5:12-21. We're condemned to death because of the sin of Adam, our representative. But in a parallel way we're declared righteous and receive life through the obedience of Christ, our representative.

Seven sons of Saul are killed and exposed "before the LORD" (2 Samuel **21:8-9**). The sacrificial nature of this act is highlighted at a number of points in the text. David describes it as an act of "atonement" in **verse 3**. And **verse 14** implies that God received this sacrifice, for he responds by answering prayer on behalf of the previously famine-stricken land.

The grief of Rizpah, the mother of two of the victims, in **verses 10-12**, highlights just how tragic atonement is.

Atonement can appear offensive to modern sensibilities. Our theories of atonement may make it seem quite clean and our church art may beautify it. But the atonement which lies at the heart of our salvation involved the slow, bloody death of Jesus on a crude cross of wood. It wasn't clean, nor was it beautiful. It was brutal and violent. Atonement is not an intellectual theory or clever piece of accounting or a paper transaction. It's bloody, brutal and ugly.

But mark this: *atonement is ugly because sin is ugly.* Sin presents itself to us with a beautiful mask so that we are tempted. But behind the mask is a rotting corpse. Sin is death. Death is sin in its true colours. And death is what is required for sin to be atoned for.

Verse 1 says, "There is bloodguilt on Saul and on his house" (ESV). "The wages of sin is death," says Paul in Romans 6:23. The guilt of sin requires the giving up of life, signified by the shedding of blood. There is bloodguilt. And the bloodguilt of Saul must be paid for

> Atonement is not an intellectual theory or a paper transaction. It's bloody, brutal and ugly.

through the sacrificial shedding of the blood of his sons. This principle forms the backdrop to the climax (or anti-climax) of 2 Samuel 24.

Meanwhile, Mephibosheth pops up one last time in the story of David (4:4; 16:1-4; 19:24-30; **21:7**). In 2 Samuel 21 his story acts as a foil to Saul's covenant-breaking. David deals with him graciously because of his covenant with Jonathan. But Mephibosheth also represents the house of Saul—he's Jonathan's son and Saul's grandson.

David's kindness to Mephibosheth is a sign that he's not seized the throne from Saul's family. This is reinforced by the honour he shows the house of Saul by burying Saul and his sons in an appropriate way (**v 11-14**). David keeps his covenant with Jonathan just as God keeps his covenant with David.

In 2 Corinthians 1:20 Paul says:

"No matter how many promises God has made, they are 'Yes' in Christ. And so through him the 'Amen' is spoken by us to the glory of God."

Our God is a covenant-keeping God. Like Mephibosheth with David, we can trust God to keep his promises. But in 2 Corinthians 1 Paul is making a link between God's faithfulness and ours. He's explaining to the Corinthians why he had to change his plans because he wants them to know he's committed to keeping his word. And that's important because he wants them to trust his gospel message. Christians need to have a reputation for reliability if people are going to trust our message about Jesus.

Questions for reflection

1. *"Atonement is ugly because sin is ugly."* Does the brutality of the cross offend you? Think about the reality of the atonement that Christ made for us on the cross—and be thankful.

2. *"Sin presents itself to us with a beautiful mask so that we are tempted. But behind the mask is a rotting corpse."* In what areas are you vulnerable to thinking that sin is beautiful and attractive? How can you keep alert to this deception, and so avoid it?

3. *"Christians need to have a reputation for reliability if people are going to trust our message about Jesus."* Are you true to your promises? Think about how you can model and encourage reliability in yourself and in others.

PART TWO

The Bloodguilt of David

2 Samuel 21 showed how you atone when your crime is against the Gibeonites. And it's brutal and bloody. But how do you atone when your crime is against God? That chapter 24 begins "again" suggests a link between the bloodguilt of Saul and the bloodguilt of David (**24:1**).

In **verse 2** David orders a census of the fighting men. Joab, the head of the army, objects (**v 3**). "The king's word, however, overruled Joab and the army commanders" (**v 4**). So they set out on a tour that involves travelling across the entire land (**v 4-7**) and takes over nine months (**v 8**). The results confirm that there are 800,000 fighting men from Israel and 500,000 from Judah (**v 9**). It's enough to make a king feel very secure. Under David, Israel was the superpower of the day. As 2 Samuel 22 testifies, he had crushed his enemies (22:38-43) and subdued the nations (22:44-50).

But a million plus men are no protection when God is your enemy. And David's census was a sin against God. Joab realised that straight away (**24:3**) and David did as soon as it was finished (**v 10**). Then the prophet Gad is sent to announce God's judgment (**v 11-13**).

It's not clear, however, *why* it was sinful. Taking a census was not inherently wrong, as God himself initiated a census in Numbers 1:1-3. The book of Numbers takes its name from that census. David's census may have been sinful because it was an expression of misplaced confidence. Perhaps David had begun to think the kingdom would only be secure if he had a large army, when in reality the kingdom of God is built on the promise of God. Perhaps his anxiety about numbers revealed a lack of trust in God.

An additional explanation of David's crime may lie in echoes of the exodus found in this passage. The word for "plague" in 2 Samuel **24:21** and **25** is the word used for the plagues on Egypt during the exodus (Exodus 7 – 12). And, just as at the Passover, only a sacrifice can avert the plague of death. If David's punishment was **analogous** to that of Pharaoh, then maybe so was his crime. And Pharaoh's first crime was to use God's people as slaves. Instead of respecting them as belonging to God, he took them as his own. In another defining moment in his reign, David took another man's wife as his own (2 Samuel 11 – 12). Now he takes the people belonging to God and treats them as his own possession. We are told in 20:24 that "Adoniram was in charge of forced labour".

A Strange Twist

But there is a strange twist. In **24:1** we're told that not only was the census a *cause* of God's anger; it was also a *result* of God's anger:

> "Again the anger of the LORD burned against Israel, and he incited David against them, saying, 'Go and take a census of Israel and Judah.'"

We don't know what it was that caused this initial divine anger. More puzzling still, we don't *why* God incited David to commit a further crime that led to judgment. Why not simply judge Israel for whatever it was that initially provoked God's anger in **verse 1**? Perhaps the reason is that the census created a clear example of the self-confidence that had originally provoked God's anger. Instead of looking to God, the people were trusting in their military might. That needed to be remedied. An accusation of misplaced self-confidence is somewhat vague. It's hard to provide chapter and verse when someone asks, "When did I do that?" But the census meant this hidden attitude was now out in the open.

So judgment is pronounced (**v 11-13**), but David must choose the form in which it comes:

- three years of famine,

- three months of enemy attack, or...

- three days of plague.

David replies in **verse 14**:

"I am in deep distress. Let us fall into the hands of the LORD, for
his mercy is great; but do not let me fall into the hands of men."

David gives the choice back to God (perhaps thereby ruling out the
option of being overrun by enemies for three months). He is confident
that God will exercise judgment with mercy.

We sometimes talk about there being one thing worse than falling
into the hands of an enemy, and that is to fall into the hands of the
living God. This is true because you cannot *escape* from God and you
cannot *defeat* God. But it's also true that God's judgment is measured
and merciful. Yes, his judgment is eternal and terrible. But God is not
a torturer. He's not a malignant force venting unrestrained anger. Even
in hell his judgment will be measured and appropriate.

Nevertheless there is judgment and it is terrible. Seventy thousand
people die as the plague spreads across the country from Dan to Beer-
sheba (**v 15**).

But then we read in **verse 16**:

"When the angel stretched out his hand to destroy Jerusalem, the
LORD relented concerning the disaster and said to the angel who
was afflicting the people, 'Enough! Withdraw your hand.' The
angel of the LORD was then at
the threshing-floor of Araunah
the Jebusite."

You can almost imagine the
plague as a dark cloud spreading
its shadow across the land until
it approaches Jerusalem. Then it
stops. David's confidence in God's
mercy is vindicated. God "relents" and withdraws the angel before it
reaches Jerusalem.

> There must be
> judgment, for God
> is just. The wrong
> must be put right.

But there *must be judgment* for God is just. If judgment is to be
exercised with mercy, there must be atonement. The wrong must be
put right. And so we read in **verse 18**, "On that day Gad went to
David and said to him, 'Go up and build an altar to the LORD on the

threshing-floor of Araunah the Jebusite.'" David is told to offer sacrifices at the specific place outside Jerusalem where the angel halted. So David buys the land, making sure that everything is done correctly (**v 19-24**). There can be no shortcuts, or attempts at cost-saving. The full price must be paid (**v 24**).

> "David built an altar to the LORD there and sacrificed burnt offerings and fellowship offerings. Then the LORD answered his prayer on behalf of the land, and the plague on Israel was stopped." (**v 25**)

The point is this: *the plague stops because of sacrifice*. Seventy thousand people have died. More people deserve to die. But instead an animal dies in their place. It's still bloody and it's still brutal. But it's an animal dying in the place of the people. This is God's mercy.

A Significant Place

This is a significant place and a significant moment. 2 Chronicles 3:1 tells us that the threshing-floor of Araunah was the very spot where a thousand years earlier Abraham had offered his son Isaac. God had told him to sacrifice Isaac at a place called Mount Moriah. But, as Abraham raised his hand, God had intervened and provided a ram as a substitute. The ram died in the place of Isaac. Now at the very same spot, God's hand is again raised against his people. But again he withdraws it (2 Samuel **24:16**). Again there is a substitute. Sacrifice is made in place of the people.

And that's not all. 2 Chronicles 3:1 also tells us that the threshing-floor of Araunah was also the place where Solomon built the temple. This spot became the central and permanent place of sacrifice. This was where the Israelites could come to find atonement with God. This was the place where sacrifices were made in place of the people.

The problem is this: the sacrifice of animals can never truly deal with sin or avert judgment. These deaths were only ever an illustration of what was to come. The most haunting words of this chapter, and the key to understanding why this incident is the climax of 2 Samuel, are David's words in verse **24:17**:

"When David saw the angel who was striking down the people, he said to the LORD, 'I have sinned. I, the shepherd, have done wrong. These are but sheep. What have they done? Let your hand fall on me and my family.'"

David sees the angel striking down the people and he's heartbroken. He cannot bear to see it. So he offers himself: *Let me take the judgment. Let your hand on fall on my family.*

And God relents. Judgment is suspended. But that prayer hangs over the house of David. It's awaiting an answer. It's a prayer that haunts history. *These are but sheep. I am the shepherd. Let your hand fall on me and my family.*

Then a thousand years later Jesus says, "I am the good shepherd. The good shepherd lays down his life for the sheep" (John 10:11). Jesus says in effect, *I am the Son of David. Let your hand fall upon me.* Jesus sees the judgment of God hanging over the people of God, hanging over you. And he's heartbroken. He cannot bear to see it. So he offers himself as the sacrifice. *Let your hand fall on me*, says Jesus. Moreover, the Son is the revelation of the Father. To see the Son is to see the Father. This is the mercy of God, and "his mercy is great" (2 Samuel **24:14**).

So it is that, a thousand years later, the prayer was answered. The hand of God's judgment did indeed fall on David's offspring on this same spot—on Mount Moriah, at the threshing-floor of Araunah, near the temple of Solomon, as Jesus hung on the cross. Once again a father's hand was raised—just it had been over Isaac. But this time it was not withdrawn. There was no alternative. Once again the Father's hand was raised—just as it had been over Jerusalem. But this time it was not withdrawn. There was no substitute for the sacrifice. This *is* the sacrifice. Jesus is the sacrifice to

> Jesus is the sacrifice to which all the other sacrifices of history have pointed.

which all the other sacrifices of history have pointed. He is the one who died in our place.

The judgment of God fell on Jesus. And through that judgment, judgment is averted from God's people.

Isaac was spared after a journey of three days. Jerusalem was spared after a plague of three days. And after three days Jesus rose from the dead. The judgment of God fell on Jesus and extinguished the life of Jesus. But three days later the judgment was gone. Your judgment is gone—if you put yourself in his hands.

The End

What an ending! Why would you end this book in any other way than this?

The novel *Revelation* by C. J. Sansom depicts a young man in Bedlam hospital for the insane. This young man knows he's a sinner and he knows God is holy. So he has been driven mad with fear. Yet in some ways his reaction is sane. It is sanity to be overcome with fear at the prospect of divine judgment. It is sanity—unless you know that God himself has atoned for your sin. We all still have those moments of sane madness. We can be anxious or weighed down by guilt or desperate to prove ourselves because we forget that God himself has atoned.

Remember David is "the christ", God's anointed king, who points forward to the Christ, Jesus. "I [am] the shepherd," says the christ. "These are but sheep ... Let your hand fall on me" (**v 17**). "Let us fall into the hands of the LORD, for his mercy is great" (**v 14**). Fall into the hands of the LORD. Stop trying to self-atone. Stop trying to self-harm. Stop trying to prove yourself. Fall into the hands of God, for his mercy is great.

Questions for reflection

1. David is guilty, but makes the right choice when the LORD gives him three choices. Think through what choice you might have made in the same circumstances. What can we learn about our own decision-making from this?

2. Our atonement is complete in the costly death of Jesus. How will this truth help us when we feel guilty, or if we are tempted to slip into old habits of sin?

3. What are the big things that have stayed with you from the book of 2 Samuel? If you could sum these up for yourself, what have you learned about God and our response to him? How will you be changed by these truths?

GLOSSARY

Abel: Adam and Eve's second son. When God accepted Abel's offering and not that of his brother, Cain, Cain killed his brother (see Genesis 4:1-16).

Abimelek: a judge (leader) of Israel who was killed when a woman dropped a stone on his head from a tower (Judges 9).

Abraham: (also called Abram) the ancestor of the nation of Israel, and the man God made a binding agreement (covenant) with. God promised to make his family into a great nation, give them a land, and bring blessing to all nations through one of his descendants (see Genesis 12:1-3).

Accession: when a king or queen takes up their power by being enthroned, often in a formal ceremony.

Agrarian: an economy and culture based on farming.

Amalekite: a member of a nomadic desert tribe from Moab; descendants of Amalek, a grandson of Esau.

Ammonite: a tribe descended from Abraham's nephew Lot who were antagonistic to Israel. Their main city was Rabbah to the south of Syria.

Analogous: comparable in certain respects, typically in a way which makes things clearer.

Anarchy: a state of disorder due to the absence or non-recognition of authority.

Angels: spiritual beings created by God to be his servants. The name means "messenger". Angels often appear in the Bible to give special or significant messages to people from God, or to dispense God's judgment.

Anoint: the act of pouring oil on someone's head to show that they have been chosen and marked by God for a special task, e.g. kingship.

Apologetics: to make a reasoned argument or statement in defence of Christian truth.

Apostasy: the act of abandoning a profession of faith or departing from your religion's beliefs and practices.

Arameans: A member of the Aramaic-speaking people that lived in Aram (modern Syria). Their chief city was Damascus.

Ark of the Covenant: a chest which contained the tablets inscribed with the ten commandments (Exodus 25). It was a symbol of God's presence with the Israelites.

Arsenal: an English football club based in North London.

Augustine: An influential Christian thinker (AD 354-430) who was Bishop of Hippo in North Africa. His writings, such as *Confessions* and *City of God* were a strong influence on Western Christianity.

Baals: pagan false gods that were worshipped by the Canaanites living around Israel.

Bathsheba: wife of Uriah the Hittite, who was seduced by King David, and eventually became his wife.

Benjamin: youngest son of Jacob, whose offspring became the smallest tribe of Israel.

Benjaminites: members of the tribe of Benjamin.

Body Politic: the people of a nation, state, or society considered collectively as an organized group of citizens.

Canaanite: inhabitants of the area west of the River Jordan who were defeated when Israel claimed the promised land.

Canon: the official list of Bible books that are accepted as genuine.

Chelsea: an English football team based in west London.

Cherubim: a type of angel—God's warrior-messengers.

Chiastic: a literary device in which words or ideas are repeated in reverse order.

Choreography: a sequence of steps and movements in a dance.

Chronological: in time order.

Chrysostom: an important leader in the early church (AD 347-407), the Bishop of Constantinople. He attempted to reform corruption in the court, clergy and the people. His name means "golden-mouthed".

Circus: in ancient Rome, a rounded or oval arena lined with seats and used for horse-and-chariot racing, and other games and sports.

City of Refuge: The Cities of Refuge were six Levitical towns in the in which people could claim the right of asylum, if they had killed someone. Their lives were safe until a court decided if the death they caused was intentional (murder) or unintentional (manslaughter).

Concubine: a woman who lives with a man but who has a lower status than his wife (or wives); a sort of official live-in lover.

Coup: the sudden, violent and illegal seizure of power from a government or king.

Covenant: a binding agreement between two parties. Often used to refer to *the* covenant that God made at Sinai with and on behalf of his people.

Dagon: a deity worshipped by the Philistines, represented as a fish-tailed man.

Damascus: the major city of the Arameans. Capital of modern Syria.

Daniel: Jewish prophet who lived during Israel's exile in Babylon.

De facto: Latin phrase meaning "in fact"; the reality of the matter, whether it is intended or not.

Doctrinal: concerned with doctrine—statements of what is true about God.

Dynasty: a number of hereditary rulers in a country. Dynasties are often named after the first king, so the Davidic dynasty is made up of all the kings and rulers descended from David who ruled in Judah.

Edom: a region south of the Dead Sea inhabited by Edomites, descendants of Esau.

Eli: a priest who served the Lord in the tabernacle at Shiloh, where he took the boy Samuel as an apprentice.

Ephod: a special tunic worn by priests while they were ministering in the temple (see Exodus 28).

Excommunicate: to officially exclude someone from participation in church life.

Exile: a time when the Jewish people were deported from their homeland to live in Babylon. This was a punishment by God for their unfaithfulness.

Exodus: literally "way out" or "departure"; the historical period when the people of Israel left slavery in Egypt and began to travel towards the promised land (i.e. the events recounted, unsurprisingly, in the book of Exodus).

Expedient: an action motivated by convenience rather than morality.

Fell: the fall is a special term for the moment when Eve and Adam disobeyed God and ate from the tree of the knowledge of good and evil (see Genesis 3).

Figuratively: not literally; language that uses pictures or metaphors to make a point.

Fratricide: the act of killing your brother.

Gath: a Philistine city; the birthplace of Goliath.

Gazelle: a small, slender antelope with curved horns.

Genocide: attempting to destroy an entire race of people.

Gentile: someone who is not Jewish.

Hamstringing: a way of crippling a horse by cutting the tendons in the leg, often used in warfare.

Hannah: the mother of the prophet Samuel. She was originally in-fertile but prayed to the Lord for a child, and he granted her Samuel.

Hebron: a city on the west bank of the Jordan river; the home of Abraham.

Hezekiah: the son of Ahaz and the 13th king of Judah. His story is told in the book of 2 Kings, and he is listed in the genealogy of Jesus in Matthew chapter 1.

Hittite: member of the Hittite empire, a war-like society, which flourished in Asia Minor (modern Turkey) and Syria from c.1700-1200 BC.

Horn: a deer's antler; often used metaphorically in the Bible to symbolise the strength of a king.

Hyperbole: an exaggerated statement or claim that is used for emphasis, and is not meant to be taken literally.

Hyssop: a small, bushy, aromatic plant with bitter minty leaves used in cooking and medicine. It's twigs were used for sprinkling water in purification rites.

Idiom: an expression that is natural to a language, that has a meaning different from its literal sense, e.g. "over the moon".

Impunity: an act done without fear of any punishment or consequences.

Isaac: one of the **patriarchs**.

Jebusites: inhabitants of Jebus, which became Jerusalem after David conquered the city.

Jesse: the father of David.

Jonathan: the son of Saul, and close friend of David.

Joshua: leader of the people of Israel after Moses. One of only two people who were both rescued from slavery in Egypt and also set foot in the promised land of Canaan.

Judges: leaders of Israel after the death of Joshua and before Saul was made king. Their stories are told in the book of Judges.

Kohathites: descendents of Levi who served in the tabernacle and the temple as assistants to the priests.

Lament: a song expressing grief or sorrow.

Levi: one of the 12 sons of Jacob; he gave his name to the tribe of Levi, whose men became assistants to the priests in Jewish worship.

Machiavellian: cunning, scheming and unscrupulous, especially in politics. Named after Niccolo Machiavelli, the author of an Italian manual on politics that described and encouraged such behaviour.

Maelstrom: a powerful whirlpool; the word is used as a metaphor to describe any situation that is confused or in violent turmoil.

Manna: the "bread" that God miraculously provided each morning for the Israelites to eat while they were journeying to the promised land (see Exodus 16). It looked like white flakes.

Melchizedek: a priest and king of Salem (which became Jerusalem). He was revered by Abraham, who paid tithes to him (Genesis 14:18).

Michal: the younger daughter of Saul; she married David.

Moabites: members of the people living in Moab, east of the River Jordan, descended from Lot.

Mosaic: relating to the Old Testament laws, which God gave Moses in the books of Exodus, Leviticus, Numbers and Deuteronomy, and which lay out how Israel were to relate to God and live as his people.

Moses: the leader of God's people at the time when God brought them out of slavery in Egypt. God communicated his law (including the Ten Commandments) through Moses, and under his leadership guided them towards the land he had promised to give them.

Motif: a repeated idea in music, imagery or language.

Nehemiah: a Jewish official in the Persian court who oversaw the return of a group of Israelites to Jerusalem after their exile in Babylon, and the rebuilding of the city's walls.

Nexus: a connection, or a series of connections, linking two or more things.

Pandora's box: a greek myth. Pandora, wife of Prometheus, is given a box filled with evil, which she must not open. But one day she does, and once opened, the evil it contains spreads out into the world.

Parable: a memorable story told to illustrate a truth.

Patriarchs: the main characters in the Genesis story: Abraham, Isaac and Jacob, their forefathers, and the sons of Jacob.

Personification: a literary device where human or personal characteristics are attached to something that is not human.

Philistia, Philistine: the country and the people from a region to the south-east of Israel.

Phinehas: one of the wayward sons of Eli.

Pincer movement: a classic military tactic where two bodies of troops converge upon an enemy.

Plunder: to steal goods during a time of disorder or war. The goods taken can be called "plunder".

Polygamy: having more than one wife at the same time.

Prodigal: a wasteful person; spending money recklessly or lavishly.

Protagonists: the leading characters in a story.

Providence: The protective care and power of God, who directs everything for the good of his people.

Puritan: a member of a sixteenth- and seventeenth-century movement in Great Britain which was committed to the Bible as God's word, to simpler worship services, to greater commitment and devotion to following Christ, and increasingly, to resisting the institutional church's hierarchical structures. Many emigrated to what would become the US, and were a strong influence on the church in most of the early colonies.

quid pro quo: a Latin phrase (literally, *something for something*) meaning a favour or advantage granted in return for something else.

Raca: an Aramaic insult, meaning "idiot" or "fool".

Redemption: the act of freeing or releasing someone; buying someone back for a price.

Regicide: killing a king.

Rhetorical question: a questioning technique used by a speaker or writer to try to persuade the listener or reader to see an issue in a different way. A question that is asked, to which the answer is obvious, and does not need saying.

Sabbath: Saturday; the holy day when Jewish people were commanded not to work (see Exodus 20:8-11).

Samson: a man who led Israel during the time of the judges, and was also born to a previously infertile woman (see Judges 13 – 16). He is most often remembered for his supernatural strength.

Satan: Hebrew name for the devil. The name means "adversary".

Samuel: son of Ahnnah and Elkanah who became the prophet who anointed David as king. His story is told in 1 Samuel.

Sanhedrin: the highest court in Israel in Jesus' and Paul's time.

Saul: the first king of Israel (see 1 Samuel 8 – 10).

Scavenging: searching for useful things, especially food, from discarded waste.

Shadrach, Meshach and Abednego: three faithful Jewish men who were put into a fiery furnace by Nebuchadnezzar (Daniel 3).

Succession: the action of inheriting a title or property, especially kingship. The new king is said to "succeed" the old king.

Syllables: units of pronunciation having a single vowel sound.

Tabernacle: a large, tented area where the Israelites worshipped God, and where his presence symbolically dwelled (see Exodus 26; 40).

Tekoa: a town to the south of Jerusalem.

Thematic: organised according to a theme.

Torah: the law of God as revealed to Moses.

Tribute: regular payments made by one state to another after they have been defeated. A kind of tax, or protection money.

Tyrant: a cruel and oppressive ruler.

Usurpation: to take a position of power illegally or by force.

Whet: to sharpen a blade.

Yahweh: the name by which God revealed himself to Moses (Exodus 3:13-14). Literally, it means, "I am who I am" or, "I will be who I will be." Most English-language Bibles translate it as "LORD."

Ziklag: a desert town in the Negev region in the south-west of Judah.

Zion, Mount Zion: another name for Jerusalem (more specifically, the mountain upon which it was built).

Zobah: an important Aramean city south of Damascus.

APPENDIX: 1 and 2 Samuel and the Psalms

Here is a list of psalms explicitly linked to the life of David in 1 and 2 Samuel by their superscription or content.

Psalm 3	David's flight from Absalom	2 Samuel 15 –16
Psalm 18	David's deliverance from Saul	1 Samuel 23 – 27
Psalm 34	David pretends to be mad	1 Samuel 21
Psalm 51	David is confronted over his adultery	2 Samuel 11 – 12
Psalm 52	David's betrayal by Doeg	1 Samuel 22
Psalm 54	David's betrayal by the Ziphites	1 Samuel 23
Psalm 56	David seized at Gath by the Philistines	1 Samuel 21
Psalm 57	David's escape from Saul into the cave	1 Samuel 22
Psalm 59	David's escape when Saul sends men to his house	1 Samuel 19
Psalm 60	David's wars with the Arameans and Edomites	2 Samuel 8 – 10
Psalm 63	David in the Desert of Judah	1 Samuel 23 – 24
Psalm 78	God's covenant with David	2 Samuel 7
Psalm 89	God's covenant with David	2 Samuel 7
Psalm 132	God's covenant with David	2 Samuel 7
Psalm 142	David's escape from Saul into the cave	1 Samuel 22

1 Samuel 19	David's escape when Saul sends men to his house	Psalm 59
1 Samuel 21	David pretends to be mad	Psalm 34
1 Samuel 21	David seized at Gath by the Philistines	Psalm 56
1 Samuel 22	David's betrayal by Doeg	Psalm 52
1 Samuel 22	David's escape from Saul into the cave	Psalm 57
1 Samuel 22	David's escape from Saul into the cave	Psalm 142
1 Samuel 23	David's betrayal by the Ziphites	Psalm 54
1 Samuel 23 – 24	David in the Desert of Judah	Psalm 63
1 Samuel 23 – 27	David's deliverance from Saul	Psalm 18
2 Samuel 11 – 12	David is confronted over his adultery	Psalm 51
2 Samuel 15 –16	David's flight from Absalom	Psalm 3
2 Samuel 7	God's covenant with David	Psalm 78
2 Samuel 7	God's covenant with David	Psalm 89
2 Samuel 7	God's covenant with David	Psalm 132
2 Samuel 8 – 10	David's wars with the Arameans and Edomites	Psalm 60

Appendix: Map of Israel in the time of 1 & 2 Samuel

BIBLIOGRAPHY

The works by Peter Leithart and John Woodhouse are particularly recommended:

■ Robert Alter, *Ancient Israel: The Former Prophets: Joshua, Judges, Samuel, and Kings* (W. W. Norton, 2013)

■ Robert D. Bergen, *1, 2 Samuel*, New American Commentary (Broadman, 1996)

■ Walter Brueggemann, *First and Second Samuel, Interpretation* (John Knox Press, 1990)

■ Dale Ralph Davis, *2 Samuel: Out of Every Adversity,* Focus on the Bible (Christian Focus, 1999)

■ David G. Firth, *1 & 2 Samuel,* Apollos Old Testament Commentary (Apollos/InterVarsity, 2009)

■ John R. Franke (ed.), *Joshua, Judges, Ruth, 1 & 2 Samuel*, Ancient Christian Commentary on Scripture: Old Testament Volume IV (InterVarsity Press, 2005)

■ Peter J. Leithart, *A Son to Me: An Exposition of 1 & 2 Samuel* (Canon Press, 2003)

■ Andrew Reid, *1 and 2 Samuel: Hope for the Helpless* (Aquila, 2008).

■ John Woodhouse, *2 Samuel: Your Kingdom Come,* Preaching the Word (Crossway, 2015)

2 Samuel for...
Bible-study Groups

Tim Chester's **Good Book Guide** to 2 Samuel is the companion to this resource, helping groups of Christians to explore, discuss and apply the book together. Seven studies, each including investigation, apply, getting personal, pray and explore more sections, take you through the main themes of the book. Includes a concise Leader's Guide at the back.

God's Word For You Series

- **Exodus For You**
  Tim Chester

- **Judges For You**
  Timothy Keller

- **Ruth For You**
  Tony Merida

- **1 Samuel For You**
  Tim Chester

- **2 Samuel For You**
  Tim Chester

- **Psalms For You**
  Christopher Ash

- **Proverbs For You**
  Kathleen Nielson

- **Daniel For You**
  David Helm

- **Micah For You**
  Stephen Um

- **Luke 1-12 For You**
  Mike McKinley

- **Luke 12-24 For You**
  Mike McKinley

- **John 1-12 For You**
  Josh Moody

- **John 13-21 For You**
  Josh Moody

- **Acts 1-12 For You**
  Albert Mohler

- **Acts 13-28 For You**
  Albert Mohler

- **Romans 1-7 For You**
  Timothy Keller

- **Romans 8-16 For You**
  Timothy Keller

- **1 Corinthians For You**
  Andrew Wilson

- **2 Corinthians For You**
  Gary Millar

- **Galatians For You**
  Timothy Keller

- **Ephesians For You**
  Richard Coekin

- **Philippians For You**
  Steven Lawson

- **Colossians & Philemon For You**
  Mark Meynell

- **1 & 2 Timothy For You**
  Phillip Jensen

- **Titus For You**
  Tim Chester

- **Hebrews For You**
  Michael Kruger

- **James For You**
  Sam Allberry

- **1 Peter For You**
  Juan Sanchez

- **Revelation For You**
  Tim Chester

Find out more at:
www.thegoodbook.com/for-you

BIBLICAL | RELEVANT | ACCESSIBLE

At The Good Book Company, we are dedicated to helping Christians and local churches grow. We believe that God's growth process always starts with hearing clearly what he has said to us through his timeless word—the Bible.

Ever since we opened our doors in 1991, we have been striving to produce Bible-based resources that bring glory to God. We have grown to become an international provider of user-friendly resources to the Christian community, with believers of all backgrounds and denominations using our books, Bible studies, devotionals, evangelistic resources, and DVD-based courses.

We want to equip ordinary Christians to live for Christ day by day, and churches to grow in their knowledge of God, their love for one another, and the effectiveness of their outreach.

Call us for a discussion of your needs or visit one of our local websites for more information on the resources and services we provide.

Your friends at The Good Book Company

thegoodbook.com | thegoodbook.co.uk
thegoodbook.com.au | thegoodbook.co.nz
thegoodbook.co.in